DEADLY DISEASES AND EPIDEMICS

BOTULISM

Second Edition

Donald Emmeluth, Ed.D.

CONSULTING EDITOR
Hilary Babcock, M.D., M.P.H.,
Infectious Diseases Division,
Washington University School of Medicine,
Medical Director of Occupational Health (Infectious Diseases),
Barnes-Jewish Hospital and St. Louis Children's Hospital

FOREWORD BY
David Heymann
World Health Organization

CHELSEA HOUSE
P U B L I S H E R S
An imprint of Infobase Publishing

Botulism, Second Edition

Chelsea House
An imprint of Infobase Publishing
132 West 31st Street
New York NY 10001

Library of Congress Cataloging-in-Publication Data

Emmeluth, Donald.
  Botulism / Donald Emmeluth ; consulting editor, Hilary Babcock ; foreword by David L. Heymann. — 2nd ed.
      p. cm. — (Deadly diseases and epidemics)
  Includes bibliographical references and index.
  ISBN-13: 978-1-60413-235-9 (hardcover : alk. paper)
  ISBN-10: 1-60413-235-3 (hardcover : alk. paper) 1. Botulism. I. Title. II. Series.

  RC143.E46 2010
  616.9'315—dc22

                          2010008111

Chelsea House books are available at special discounts when purchased in bulk quantities for businesses, associations, institutions, or sales promotions. Please call our Special Sales Department in New York at (212) 967-8800 or (800) 322-8755.

You can find Chelsea House on the World Wide Web at
http://www.chelseahouse.com

Text design by Terry Mallon
Illustrations by Sholto Ainslie
Cover design by Takeshi Takahashi
Composition by Mary Susan Ryan-Flynn
Cover printed by Bang Printing, Brainerd, MN
Book printed and bound by Bang Printing, Brainerd, MN
Date printed: May 2010
Printed in the United States of America

10 9 8 7 6 5 4 3 2 1

This book is printed on acid-free paper.

All links and Web addresses were checked and verified to be correct at the time of publication. Because of the dynamic nature of the Web, some addresses and links may have changed since publication and may no longer be valid.

Table of Contents

Foreword 6

1. Introduction 8

2. Historical Perspective 16

3. Causes of Botulism 28

4. Transmission of Botulism 41

5. Diagnosis of Botulism 49

6. Botulism and the Nervous System 59

7. Treating Botulism 71

8. Preventing Botulism 82

9. Concerns for the Future:
   Botulism and Bioterrorism 92

10. Hopes for the Future 107

Notes 120

Glossary 122

Bibliography 126

Further Resources 136

Index 138

Foreword

Communicable diseases kill and cause long-term disability. The microbial agents that cause them are dynamic, changeable, and resilient: They are responsible for more than 14 million deaths each year, mainly in developing countries.

Approximately 46 percent of all deaths in the developing world are due to communicable diseases, and almost 90 percent of these deaths are from AIDS, tuberculosis, malaria, and acute diarrheal and respiratory infections of children. In addition to causing great human suffering, these high-mortality communicable diseases have become major obstacles to economic development. They are a challenge to control either because of the lack of effective vaccines, or because the drugs that are used to treat them are becoming less effective because of antimicrobial drug resistance.

Millions of people, especially those who are poor and living in developing countries, are also at risk from disabling communicable diseases such as polio, leprosy, lymphatic filariasis, and onchocerciasis. In addition to human suffering and permanent disability, these communicable diseases create an economic burden—both on the workforce that handicapped persons are unable to join, and on their families and society, upon which they must often depend for economic support.

Finally, the entire world is at risk of the unexpected communicable diseases, those that are called emerging or reemerging infections. Infection is often unpredictable because risk factors for transmission are not understood, or because it often results from organisms that cross the species barrier from animals to humans. The cause is often viral, such as Ebola and Marburg hemorrhagic fevers and severe acute respiratory syndrome (SARS). In addition to causing human suffering and death, these infections place health workers at great risk and are costly to economies. Infections such as Bovine Spongiform Encephalopathy (BSE) and the associated new human variant of Creutzfeldt-Jakob disease (vCJD) in Europe, and avian influenza A (H5N1) in Asia, are reminders of the seriousness of emerging and re-emerging infections. In addition, many of these infections have the potential to cause pandemics, which are a constant threat to our economies and public health security.

Science has given us vaccines and anti-infective drugs that have helped keep infectious diseases under control. Nothing demonstrates the effectiveness of vaccines better than the successful eradication of smallpox, the decrease in polio as the eradication program continues, and the decrease in measles when routine immunization programs are supplemented by mass vaccination campaigns.

Likewise, the effectiveness of anti-infective drugs is clearly demonstrated through prolonged life or better health in those infected with viral diseases such as AIDS, parasitic infections such as malaria, and bacterial infections such as tuberculosis and pneumococcal pneumonia.

But current research and development is not filling the pipeline for new anti-infective drugs as rapidly as resistance is developing, nor is vaccine development providing vaccines for some of the most common and lethal communicable diseases. At the same time, providing people with access to existing anti-infective drugs, vaccines, and goods such as condoms or bed nets—necessary for the control of communicable diseases in many developing countries—remains a great challenge.

Education, experimentation, and the discoveries that grow from them are the tools needed to combat high mortality infectious diseases, diseases that cause disability, or emerging and re-emerging infectious diseases. At the same time, partnerships between developing and industrialized countries can overcome many of the challenges of access to goods and technologies. This book may inspire its readers to set out on the path of drug and vaccine development, or on the path to discovering better public health technologies by applying our current understanding of the human genome and those of various infectious agents. Readers may likewise be inspired to help ensure wider access to those protective goods and technologies. Such inspiration, with pragmatic action, will keep us on the winning side of the struggle against communicable diseases.

David L. Heymann
Assistant Director General
Health Security and Environment
Representative of the Director General for Polio Eradication
World Health Organization
Geneva, Switzerland

1

Introduction

According to the Centers for Disease Control and Prevention (CDC), about 76 million people become ill in the United States every year from eating food that is contaminated with disease-producing organisms or their products. These organisms are called **pathogens**, and the poisonous products they produce are called **toxins**. The most common of the pathogens are bacteria, but viruses and various worm **parasites** are also pathogens. Symptoms can range from the ambiguous upset stomach to fever, diarrhea, vomiting, and the associated dehydration from fluid loss. Happily, only a small percentage of people with foodborne illnesses die from them; the CDC estimates there are about 5,000 deaths annually worldwide. Raw and undercooked foods are the most common sources for these pathogens. However, contamination can occur while preparing, shipping, processing, harvesting, or growing the foods. This book will consider one type of foodborne illness known as **botulism**. Botulism is caused by a bacterium called *Clostridium botulinum,* producing deadly protein toxins that can cause paralysis or death.

TYPES OF BOTULISM

The three main clinical presentations of botulism include **infant botulism** (IB), foodborne botulism (FBB), and **wound botulism** (WB). Additionally, because of the potency of the toxin, the possibility of botulism as a bioterrorism agent or biological weapon is a great concern.

In the United States, approximately 154 cases of botulism are reported annually to the Centers for Disease Control and Prevention (CDC). Infant botulism accounts for nearly 75 percent of all botulism cases. The incidence of foodborne botulism is approximately 24 cases per year. The incidence of

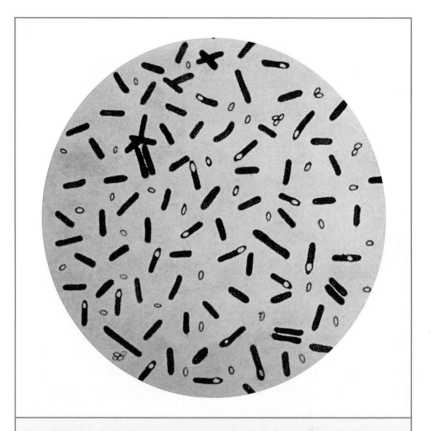

Figure 1.1 *Clostridium botulinum* (seen here) is a rod-shaped bacterium that can produce an endospore near one end of its cell. This picture also depicts a number of free endospores (small circles) that remain when the vegetative portion of the cell dies away. (Centers for Disease Control and Prevention [CDC])

wound botulism is 3 cases per year. The incidence of infant botulism is 71 cases per year, with a mean age of 3 months.

Toxin A is found predominantly west of the Mississippi River. Toxin B is found most commonly in the eastern United States. Toxin E is found in northern latitudes, such as the Pacific Northwest, the Great Lakes region, and Alaska. The frequency of botulism in native Alaskans is among the highest in the world. Toxin E outbreaks are frequently associated with fish products.

Human botulism is found worldwide. Spores from *C botulinum* strains that produce type A or B toxins are distributed widely in the soil and have been found throughout the world. Toxin type B is commonly found in Europe. Toxin G was originally isolated in Switzerland.

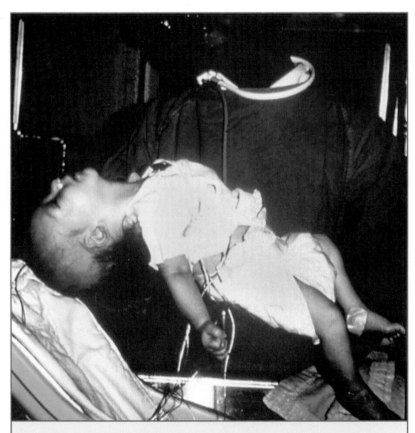

Figure 1.2 A common characteristic of infant botulism is the apparent inability of the child to hold its head upright. This is part of a syndrome of symptoms known as flaccid paralysis, which starts at the neck and works down the body. The baby in this picture has botulism and needs help to support his head. (CDC)

Perhaps the best-known type of the disease is foodborne botulism, where individuals ingest the toxins in food. This type can vary from a mild illness, to one that can be fatal within 24 hours. People of both genders and all ages are susceptible to this type of infection. As mentioned earlier, cases of foodborne botulism are related to foods that are not cooked or inadequately cooked since the toxin is inactivated or destroyed by proper heating.

One of the best publicized cases of foodborne botulism involved the Bon Vivant Company of Newark, New Jersey, and its vichyssoise (cold potato soup). More than 6,000 cans of the soup were found to be contaminated by dirt that contained the botulism endospore. Investigation by the Food and Drug Administration (FDA) found that the soup had not been properly heated during the canning process. Samuel Cochran, Jr., vice president of the Bank of New York, died in June 1971 from eating the contaminated soup. His wife, Grace Wallace Cochran, was severely affected but did not die from the affliction. A third victim, Paul McDonald, also suffered incapacitating symptoms. The resulting publicity caused the Bon Vivant Soup Company to go out of business. It subsequently returned in a reorganized fashion as Moore & Company, Inc., in 1972.

One of the consequences of the Bon Vivant incident was to add importance to an industry-wide food safety initiative that began in the food processing industry in the 1960s. The initiative was developed to ensure that food taken into space by the astronauts would not be contaminated and would be safe for consumption under the conditions presented by space travel. The initiative eventually was called Hazard Analysis and Critical Control Points (HACCP) and was approved by the regulatory, scientific, and industrial partners. The Bon Vivant incident became the impetus for extending the original NASA initiative into one that impacted food for all people, not just astronauts.

Figure 1.3 Birds infected with type C botulism toxin show the same type of progressive paralysis as found in infant botulism. In birds, this is called limberneck, which often leads to death due to suffocation since the windpipe is blocked. (© AP Images)

Wound botulism occurs when contaminated soil gets into an open wound. Fewer than 5% of all botulism cases are of this type, and it tends to occur more frequently in young boys. The soil is naturally contaminated with the botulism organism.

The third type, infant botulism, is considered the most common and may be one cause of sudden infant death (Figure 1.4). Most infants are less than 6 months of age when they are infected. Contaminated honey, which has been used to sweeten milk or pacifiers, is the most common source of the infection. The honey is often contaminated with wind-borne forms of the botulism organism.

A fourth type of botulism is sometimes recognized. When a large number of the botulism organisms grow and reproduce in the intestines, the condition is called **intestinal colonization**. When bacteria grow within pockets of the intestine where oxygen concentration is low to nonexistent, they release their waste

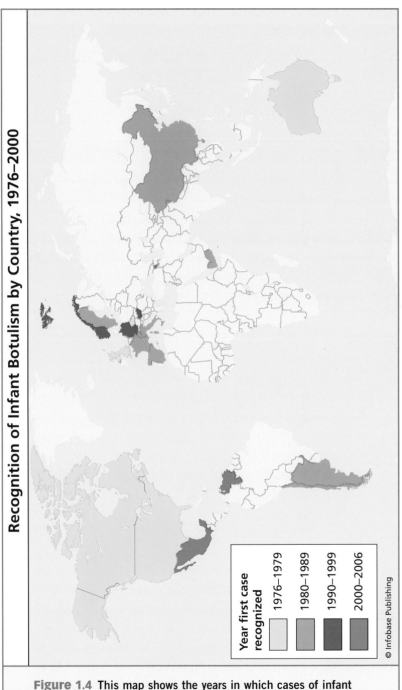

Figure 1.4 This map shows the years in which cases of infant botulism were first recognized, by country.

Table 1.1 Cases of Botulism by State and Type (Top Ten)

January 1, 2001 – December 31, 2007	
State	**Number of Cases**
California	240
Pennsylvania	95
New Jersey	41
Maryland	21
Delaware	18
Texas	18
Utah	17
Washington	15
Arizona	13
Oregon	10
http://www.cdc.gov/nationalsurveillance/botulism_surveillance.html	

products, which are toxic to the host, directly into the intestine. From there the toxin is absorbed directly into the bloodstream. This intestinal colonization of adults may lead to a toxin production and produce a situation similar to infant botulism. This condition is known as adult infectious botulism. In spite of the name, the disease is not spread from person to person. People only acquire this type of botulism by eating contaminated foods or by drug injection.

In recent years, unsuccessful attempts were made by a Japanese cult to aerosolize (turn into a fine mist that can easily spread through the air and be inhaled) *C. botulinum* toxins for use in bioterrorism attacks. **Bioterrorism** is often defined as any actual or threatened use of microorganisms or their products (toxins) designed to cause death or disease in animals, humans, or plants. In 1995, Iraq made it known that it had produced a significant amount of *C. botulinum* toxin and had the capability to produce a great deal more. There is no evidence that Iraq or any other country has carried out a successful aerosol attack. Because the toxins are unstable, the range of an aerosol attack would be limited unless delivered by a warhead from a missile. This form, known as **inhalation botulism**, does not occur naturally.

Overall, botulism is not very common. There is an average of just over 100 cases of botulism reported in the United States each year. Nearly 75% of the cases are infant botulism and about 25% are foodborne infections. However, it is important to remember that botulism can have a fatal outcome.

2

Historical Perspective

A BRIEF HISTORY OF FOOD POISONING

The sausage is thought to be among the oldest of prepared foods. Historical records suggest that the Sumerians invented sausages around 3000 B.C. in what is present-day Iraq. Homer mentions a type of sausage in the *Odyssey,* and his friend Epicharmus wrote a comedy entitled, *The Sausage.* The emperor Nero, known for making things hot for the Romans, held a festival called the Lupercalia where sausages were a featured dish. The early Catholic Church, never a fan of Nero and his antics, outlawed the festival and made consumption of sausages a sin. Emperor Constantine of Rome followed the Church's edict and banned the eating of sausages. Early in the tenth century, the Byzantine Emperor Leo VI outlawed the production of blood sausages after a number of cases of food poisoning were directly associated with people who had eaten the blood sausages. In Germany, food poisoning was called "sausage poisoning."

Southern Germany, 1817–1822

Justinus Kerner was district medical officer for the town of Württemberg in southern Germany. He had signed many death certificates of people who died with symptoms such as impaired breathing, difficulty with speaking and swallowing, and seeing double. Kerner suspected that some type of biological poison related to eating sausages caused the symptoms. Almost all of the people with these symptoms had eaten sausages that were not properly prepared and were inadequately cooked. He was able to extract a compound that he believed was the poison causing the symptoms. Between 1817 and 1822, Kerner published the first complete and accurate description of what he called *wurstgift* or "sausage poison." Today that disease is called botulism. Kerner even injected himself with the poison and caused many of the symptoms in himself. Luckily he survived, but his experiment showed a positive causal relationship between the sausage material and the disease. The disease became known as "Kerner's Disease."

The disease was not an everyday occurrence, and no large-scale **epidemics** were recognized. However, the cause of Kerner's Disease was to show up in a number of unusual situations over the next centuries.

California, 1976

Almost all of the infants affected were less than a year old. A large number of cases occurred in children who were 2 and 3 months old. They all exhibited a floppiness of their heads, as if they were too weak to hold them up. Dr. Stephen S. Arnon of the California Department of Health Services began to notice between 30 to 40 cases of the disease occurring in babies in California each year. Interestingly, a similar condition called *limberneck* shows up in ducks. This is a form of botulism in birds caused by the same *C. botulinum* organism.

The babies exhibited poor feeding, overall tiredness, and lack of attention. As parents began to track the disease, they recalled that the first symptom was usually constipation. As the disease progressed, breathing was affected; infants might eventually spend weeks or even months on a ventilator. The lack of symptoms seemed to mimic the condition known as Sudden Infant Death Syndrome (SIDS), where babies die from no obvious cause and the only symptom is the rapid unexplained death, but Dr. Arnon began to suspect that something else was the cause.

Canada began to report cases of the disease in 1979, Massachusetts reported them in 1983, and Argentina in 1984. Between 1976 and 1993, more than 1,200 cases were reported in the United States. Fortunately, the fatality rate for the disease was less than 2%.

Black Tar Heroin, 1982

Although the first heroin-related botulism cases were identified in New York City in 1982, almost all other heroin-related botulism cases have occurred in California. The symptoms of botulism were seen in injection drug users who were either skin popping (injecting heroin under the skin or into a muscle) or mainlining (injecting directly into a vein) a type of heroin called black tar heroin named for its dark, gummy appearance. The botulism symptoms began to develop within one to two days. Respiratory distress, blurred vision, and difficulty talking and swallowing all characterized the afflicted people. Drug injection gets the botulism spores into the body, leading to the symptoms of the botulism disease. Fortunately there were few deaths, and the disease remains relatively rare.

NEW CENTER PROVIDES BROADER PERSPECTIVE

Given the continuing international flavor and concern about the multifaceted problems associated with disease prevention and control, the CDC organized a new center to provide leadership in research, surveillance, and response to infectious disease. The National Center for Zoonotic, Vector-Borne, and Enteric Diseases (ZVED) was organized in April 2007. The new center attempts to provide an ecological context involving humans, animals, and plants as they interact in the complex dynamic natural environment. ZVED's mission is to improve health by using a comprehensive approach to find ways to develop healthier and safer ways to bring together human interactions with animals, animal products, wildlife, and the natural environment.

ZVED works within four divisions: the Division of Foodborne, Bacterial, and Mycotic Diseases; the Division of Parasitic Diseases; the Division of Vector-Borne Infectious Diseases; and the Division of Viral and Rickettsial Diseases.

Upstate New York, Fall 2000

The leaves were turning their rainbow of colors as the sugar maples, beeches, and yellow birch trees underwent their yearly metamorphosis. Unfortunately, this usual scene of placid beauty was transformed into a colorful graveyard vision. Along the shores of Lake Erie were scattered bodies of many species of waterfowl. The final tally showed more than 5,000 birds dead. Loons, grebes, mallard ducks, gulls, and mergansers were joined in death by a variety of fish species. In 2002, the scene was repeated along the shores of Lake Ontario. Hundreds of birds died of botulism.

IDENTIFYING THE CAUSE OF BOTULISM

The situations and circumstances described previously relate to a specific bacterial disease. The disease is botulism, and the microbe responsible is the bacterium *Clostridium botulinum*. Emile van Ermengem, professor of bacteriology at the University of Ghent, Belgium, identified this microorganism as the cause of the disease in 1895.

In 1897, there had been a botulism outbreak after a funeral dinner where smoked ham was the main course. Emile van Ermengem was called in to find the cause. In the chapters to come, we will learn more about this microorganism and how it causes the symptoms

What Kinds of Foods Are Associated with Botulism?

Almost any type of food might contain the type of botulism poison mentioned by Kerner. It is not known if the botulism poison contains the organism or merely its toxin. Only if the organism can grow in an oxygen-free environment can it release its protein toxins into the medium in which it is growing (whether this is food or a culture in a laboratory). One of the things that makes the disease so difficult to eliminate is that even salted, smoked, or vacuum-packed foods may contain the organism or its poisons. Generally, smoked or vacuum-packed foods have been improperly prepared if the poisons are present.

The most common sources of foods containing botulism toxins are home-canned or improperly canned commercial foods (Figure 2.1). The list of foods in these categories sounds like the farmers' market of produce—corn, beans of various types, asparagus, beets, and mushrooms. Even a sandwich of luncheon meats, tuna, liver pate, or smoked or salted fish is not immune to the poisons. A number of well-known outbreaks were associated with poorly prepared potato salads. The botulism organism can exist on the surface of the potato in a form that resists the temperature

HAZARD ANALYSIS AND CRITICAL CONTROL POINTS TIMELINE TABLE

1971—HACCP, as presently known, took form at the National Conference on Food Protection, where risk assessment was combined with the Critical Control Points concept.

Mid-1970s—Pillsbury first used HACCP for safety of foods in the U.S. Space Program and adopted it as a company-wide food-protection system. Pillsbury published the first comprehensive treatise on HACCP in 1973.

1973—A HACCP system was adopted for the Low-Acid Canned Food Regulations following the Bon Vivant vichyssoise soup botulism incident. (In this incident, one person died after eating the soup due to botulism poisoning.)

1985—HACCP was recommended by the National Academy of Science for broad application to various categories of non-canned food.

1989—The U.S. National Advisory Committee on Micro-biological Criteria for Food (NACMCF) developed and approved a standardized and updated HACCP system, which was endorsed by federal regulatory agencies responsible for food safety.

required for cooking the potato. Destruction of the endospore (hibernating state) form of the organism on the potato surface would require continuous boiling for more than 24 hours.

BOTULISM TODAY

In September of 2006 health officials in both Georgia and Florida received information about a total of four suspected cases of botulism. Three cases in Georgia had shared a common meal which included carrot juice from Bolthouse Farms. The Florida case also

1990s—HACCP is an internationally accepted method of ensuring food safety by identifying hazards and monitoring their Critical Control Points in the process.

December 1997—FDA's Seafood HAACP program becomes mandatory.

January 1998—HACCP becomes mandatory for large meat and poultry manufacturers.

January 1999—HACCP becomes mandatory for small meat and poultry manufacturers.

May 1999—A voluntary pilot study was initiated to test the implementation, evaluation, monitoring, and enforcement of the proposed National Conference of Interstate Milk Shipment HACCP program.

September 1999—HACCP becomes mandatory for frozen dessert manufacturers in the state of Ohio.

January 2000—HACCP becomes mandatory for very small meat and poultry manufacturers.

January 2002—The juice HACCP regulation begins to be mandatory for processors, small businesses, and very small businesses.

Figure 2.1 Improperly heated home-canned foods are the most common source of botulinum toxin. Shown here are jars of contaminated jalapeno peppers that were involved in a botulism outbreak in Michigan. (CDC)

involved carrot juice from Bolthouse. Testing showed that the bottles came from different lot numbers in the Florida and Georgia cases. Other bottles from each of the lot numbers were tested for botulinum toxin and tested negative. Proper refrigeration combined with the low acidity will normally prevent germination of the botulinum spores and production of the toxin. In both the Florida and Georgia cases the carrot juice had not been refrigerated for several hours prior to its ingestion. Two additional cases were reported from Ontario, Canada. One of the six patients died 90 days after becoming ill. After one year, two were still on ventilators and the other three had been removed from ventilators after times of three to seven months. These incidents caused the FDA to modify its guidelines for refrigerated low-acid juices to now include either acidification or appropriate heat treatment.[1]

The CDC confirmed that Uganda appeared to have a botulism outbreak to deal with. The Ugandan Minister of Health issued a warning after the death of a high school student in October of 2008. The CDC tested the dead girl and her two friends and found them contaminated with the botulinum toxin.

WHAT WOULD YOU LIKE ON YOUR HOT DOG?

Summertime in the U.S. brings thoughts of baseball, cold drinks and hot dogs, often covered with meat or chili sauce. It seems that the summer of 2007 brought more than the usual condiments to the hot dog combination. A number of cases of botulism were reported to the CDC from the end of June to the end of August. The cases were located in Ohio, Indiana and Texas. All the afflicted individuals had eaten canned hot dog chili that had been made by Castleberry Food Company. The CDC reported their initial findings to the FDA who informed Castleberry. At that point, the company instituted a voluntary recall of the chili sauce.

In mid July, the voluntary recall was expanded to over ninety products that are distributed under the Castleberry brand and other brand names including, Kroger, Food Lion and Piggly Wiggly. The recall included brands of canned dog food also. U.S. Department of Agriculture's Food Safety and Inspection Service (USDA-FSIS) joined with the FDA and the CDC in advising people not to eat any of these canned items. The recalled products list included canned chili sauce, chili, beef stew, hash, corned beef hash, barbecue pork, barbecue beef, chip beef, Brunswick stew, sausage gravy

In November of 2008, the Castleberry canning factory, located in Augusta, Georgia, closed permanently. The 2007 botulism episodes which poisoned eight people proved to be too much bad publicity for the company.[2]

Warnings were issued about purchasing canned foods that are outdated or have cans or containers that are damaged in any way. Also, foods that will be stored for long periods at room temperature should be treated carefully during preparation. The contaminated food was apparently brought in from the outside and was not part of the food being served at the high school where the girls were found. The previous cases of botulism in Uganda occurred in the 1970s.

In December of 2008, the FDA warned consumers about consuming a type of fish that had been imported into Florida from New Brunswick, Canada. Known as the alewife or gaspereaux, these fish were sold as salt-cured and ungutted. The FDA suggested that any ungutted, salt-cured, dried or smoked fish such as the alewife should be considered potentially tainted with *Clostridium botulinum*. The Florida Department of Agriculture and Consumer Services discovered the original contaminated fish and alerted the FDA which prohibited the sale of these fish in the United States.

We should remember that not all botulism cases are food related. In 2008, Dublin, Ireland was dealing with botulism among heroin users. Due to less than sanitary production methods the heroin became contaminated with botulinum spores and quickly spread among the heroin users.[3]

The official botulism Web sites of the Centers for Disease Control and Prevention (CDC) and the California Department of Public Health are suggesting that an increase in the number of wound botulism cases is due to an "epidemic" of Mexican black tar heroin abuse in California. The California Department of Public Health stated, "The number of cases of foodborne and infant botulism has changed little in recent years, but wound botulism has increased because of the injection of black tar heroin. In recent years, California has experienced an epidemic of this form of botulism and now reports nearby three-quarters of the wound botulism cases in the country."[4]

Two examples provide illustration of the need to be extremely careful when producing and using home canned vegetables. It is especially important when canning low acid foods such as green beans and asparagus. In September of 2008, a family in Ohio became infected with botulism when they consumed improperly canned green beans. A grandfather, grandmother and grandson were hospitalized and two grand-daughters were treated and released from the hospital. The grandparents are still in critical condition while the grandson is in serious condition. The grandson still faces another twelve weeks of recovery as of November 2008, considerably more for the grandparents.[5]

In February of 2009, a nurse in Spokane, Washington and her two children under ten years of age were saved from death by an emergency delivery of the anti-toxin from the Homeland Security storage facility in Seattle. The woman continues on a ventilator and has a long recovery time ahead of her. The children had milder symptoms and are recovering more rapidly. The local epidemiologist voiced concern that current economic hardships may motivate more people to can their home garden vegetables. It would seem some of them are not adhering to proper canning practice.[6]

It doesn't seem to be a good time to be part of the Stone-wall Kitchen products company. In January of 2009, the York, Maine-based company put out a warning to consumers that some of their sauces listed below may be contaminated with deadly botulism. None of these products should be eaten even though they may look or smell okay. The U.S. Food & Drug Administration (FDA) placed the following summary on its Web site:

> The following list of products was distributed nation-
> wide to consumers through the nine Stonewall Kitchen
> Company Stores, Stonewall Kitchen's direct-to-consumer
> division (catalog/internet) and through their wholesale
> division. Products could have been purchased individually

or within a gift basket. This recall affects all product codes and expiration dates for:

- Stonewall Kitchen Chocolate Hazelnut Sauce (SKU 161312) – round glass jar, 12 oz.

- Stonewall Kitchen Chocolate Peanut Butter (SKU 161211) – round glass jar, 12 oz.

- Stonewall Kitchen Coffee Caramel Sauce (SKU 161204) – round glass jar, 13 oz.

- Stonewall Kitchen Dulce de Leche Sauce (SKU 161214) – round glass jar, 12.5 oz.

- Barefoot Contessa Espresso Dulce de Leche (SKU 542313) – round glass jar, 10.5 oz.

Additionally, the following list of products was distributed nationwide to consumers through A-Hold Corporation (Stop & Shop and Giant stores). This recall affects all product codes and expiration dates for:

- Simply Enjoy Coffee Caramel Sauce – square glass jar, 13 oz.

- Simply Enjoy Chocolate Peanut Butter Sauce – square glass jar, 12 oz

Also in January of 2009, the Colorado Department of Public Health warned people across the state about the Stonewall products after the recall. The health department suggested that people in Colorado might have purchased the sauces out of a catalogue or from the Internet. In March of 2009, Health Canada warned consumers about homemade garlic-in-oil. If not stored properly it can lead to serious health issues associated with *Clostridium botulinum*. Garlic-in-oil is a mixture of oil and garlic. The garlic may be whole, chopped, or minced.

When stored at room temperature, or if refrigerated for too long, botulism spores could grow. It should be used within a week of being made and be kept in the refrigerator when not being used during that time.

Illness due to contaminated food products has become an increasing burden on the health care system here in the United States. Most of these illnesses are easily preventable by measures as simple as washing your hands. Ability to develop methods and procedures to control these problems result from a close look at the outbreaks themselves. It falls to the CDC to collect information about foodborne disease outbreaks (FBDOs) from all states and territories. This is accomplished through the Foodborne Disease Outbreak Surveillance System (FBDSS). The most recent epidemiologic data on FBDOs, which has been analyzed, is for 2006. A total of 1,270 FBDOs were reported, resulting in 27,634 cases and 11 deaths. Only one of the deaths was caused by *C. botulinum*. The findings in this report are subject to a number of limitations. Perhaps the most obvious is the fact that only a small proportion of all foodborne illnesses reported each year are identified as associated with outbreaks. Lack of funding at the state and national levels may result in a lack of diagnostic testing equipment. Whatever the reasons it is clear that there is a need to do better or more chapters on botulism will continue to be written.[7]

3

Causes of Botulism

The wedding reception had lasted long into the night. The musicians had played a number of long sets and had worked up quite a hunger and thirst. The beer and smoked ham, preserved in brine, had gone down easily. Smoked ham was a typical meat served at parties at that time. Thirty-four musicians partook of the wedding feast, and unfortunately, 23 became ill; 13 of which became severely ill. Three musicians died. It was to this setting that Emile van Ermengem of Ellezelles, Belgium, a professor at the University of Ghent, was sent. Using the techniques taught to him by his mentor Robert Koch, van Ermengem determined that a bacterium called *Bacillus botulinus* was the causative agent of the food poisoning. The organism's name was later changed to *Clostridium botulinum*.

The organism van Ermengem discovered is a strict **anaerobe**. The term *anaerobe* refers to an organism that lives in the absence of oxygen. The organism forms an endospore when conditions for its growth and survival appear compromised. Endospores are dormant survival structures formed by some bacteria. (They are discussed in greater detail later in this chapter.) Van Ermengem discovered that the toxin produced by the microbe could be destroyed if the food were cooked to at least 80°C (176°F).

WHAT ARE BACTERIA?

Living things on this planet currently are placed into five large categories called Kingdoms. There is the Plant Kingdom, Animal Kingdom, Fungi Kingdom, Protista Kingdom, and Bacteria (or Monera) Kingdom.

The cells of all living organisms are organized in one of two ways. Cells from the Plant, Animal, Fungi, and Protista Kingdoms all contain compartments constructed from internal cellular membranes. These compartments, which help to separate chemicals and other materials from the interior of the cell, are called **organelles**, or miniature organs. Organelles include the nucleus, the lysosome,

ROBERT KOCH—
FATHER OF BACTERIOLOGY

Robert Koch was a country doctor from Germany who won the Nobel Prize in Physiology or Medicine in 1905 for his body of work concerning tuberculosis and the methods for confirming its presence. He had discovered the cause of tuberculosis, a rod-shaped bacterium. Koch developed a series of protocols that allowed him to isolate pure cultures of organisms responsible for specific diseases. These protocols became known as Koch's Postulates. There are four basic steps making up these postulates. First, Koch suggested that observation should show that the same microorganism should be present in every case of a disease with the same symptoms. To confirm this observation, the second step involved isolating this microbe from the dead or diseased organism and growing it in a pure culture. Third, when a sample of that pure culture is inoculated into a test organism, the test organism should show the same symptoms as the original case of the disease. Finally, the same microorganisms should be isolated from the test subjects as were found in the original subject.

Using these common-sense protocols allowed Koch to prove Louis Pasteur's Germ Theory of Disease, which suggested that specific microorganisms were responsible for specific diseases. Pasteur was France's finest scientist and he and Koch were responsible for moving the science of microbiology from the realm of the metaphysical to the world of science. Many people who worked in Koch's lab went on to receive Nobel Prizes and other awards.

and the mitochondria. This type of cellular organization, with clearly defined and identifiable organelles, is described as the **eukaryotic** type of cellular organization. The term *eukaryotic* means "true nucleus" and comes from the Greek *eu* meaning "proper," "good," or "true," and *karyon* meaning "nucleus." Therefore, cells of plants, animals, fungi, and protozoa are known as eukaryotic cells or eukaryotes because of their internal cellular organization.

The Bacteria Kingdom includes cells with a different type of internal organization. Bacterial cells lack membrane-defined organelles, are normally smaller than eukaryotic cells, and have few clearly defined internal structures. Because bacteria lack organelles such as the nucleus, they are described as being **prokaryotic** cells. *Pro* is Greek for "before." Because bacterial cells do not have a nucleus, the genetic information (a single circular DNA molecule) resides in the cell with no membrane structure surrounding it. This type of cellular organization has served bacteria well for over 3.5 billion years.

There is another group of microorganisms that also has a prokaryotic type of cellular organization. Known as the Archaebacteria, or simply the **Archae**, they resemble bacteria in size and prokaryotic organization. However, the Archae are quite different genetically from both eukaryotic and prokaryotic types of cells. Archae contain genetic information similar to the eukaryotes and also genetic information similar to bacteria. In addition, more than 40% of their genetic information is unique, resembling neither eukaryotes nor bacteria. The Archae live in extreme environments, earning them the name "extremophiles." Extreme environments include the absence of oxygen (the term *anaerobic* describes an oxygen-free environment) or very high heat such as inside volcanoes. The first of these extremophiles was discovered in the hot springs of Yellowstone National Park by microbiologist Thomas Brock in the 1960s.

Discovery of the Archae's unique genetic makeup in the mid-1990s gave further weight to the development of a new classification scheme. All organisms are now placed into one of three groups larger than the Kingdom categories. These larger categories are called Domains. The three Domains are the Archae, the Bacteria, and the Eukarya, which includes the Plant, Animal, Protista, and Fungi Kingdoms.

Important Bacterial Structures

Bacteria were originally classified as very small plants because, like plants, they have a cell wall protecting their cell membrane and the interior of the cell. However, bacterial cell walls are made of molecules that are different from the molecules in plant cell walls. Bacterial cell walls are largely made of a molecule called **peptidoglycan**, which contains the **amino acid** peptide, and a

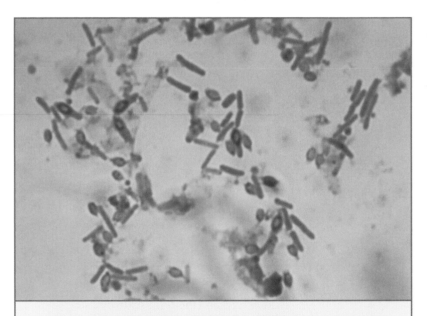

Figure 3.1 Gram-positive cells appear purple when stained using the Gram stain procedure. *Clostridium botulinum* is designated as a gram-positive rod. By combining the features of the gram reaction and the shape of the bacterial cell, microbiologists can narrow down the possible types of organisms that cause a disease. (© Dr. Arthur Siegelman/Visuals Unlimited, Inc.)

form of glucose in carbohydrates called glycan. This unique molecule is not found among eukaryotes (including humans), so the human immune system tries to remove or destroy it.

Different groups of bacteria have varying amounts of peptidoglycan in their cell wall. When treated with different dyes, these differences in the amount of peptidoglycan and other factors cause bacterial cells to retain or lose the color of specific dyes. One very famous and important staining reaction used to differentiate between bacteria is the Gram stain process. In this process, bacteria are treated with a series of different colored dyes. If the bacteria retain the first dye color (crystal violet) throughout the entire staining procedure, they look purple at the end of the test. Such bacteria are called **gram-positive bacteria**. The *C. botulinum* bacterium is gram positive (Figure 3.1). Other bacteria lose the first dye in the process and take on the color of the last dye (called the counterstain). These bacteria look pink or light red and are called **gram-negative bacteria.**

Characteristics of *C. botulinum*

Bacteria come in three basic shapes. A single bacterium shaped like a rod or a pencil is known as a **bacillus** (bacilli, plural). The botulism organism is rod-shaped. Bacteria shaped like a circle or a sphere are known as **cocci** (coccus, singular). Bacteria that are shaped like spirals or the letter "c," or are tightly wound like a spring are known as **spirilli** (spirillum, singular). Within these basic shapes, there is a great deal of variability. Rods may be long and thin or short and fat. Cocci may be more oval or egg-shaped rather than round, and spiral bacteria may range from a barely bent rod to a tightly wound spring-like structure.

Organisms for which oxygen is toxic or lethal are said to be anaerobic. *Clostridium botulinum* is considered a strict or obligatory anaerobe because it cannot tolerate any oxygen. Some anaerobes can tolerate the presence of small amounts of oxygen, which prevents their reproduction but does not kill them directly. Organisms that require oxygen in ambient air concentrations of 20–21% are said to be **aerobic.**

Endospores and Their Importance

The botulism organism is a common soil microorganism found worldwide. Dormant forms are easily spread through the air and contaminate a variety of areas. The dormant form is called an **endospore**. A limited number of bacterial groups, including *Clostridium,* have the capability of producing a highly resistant survival structure known as an endospore. This dormant structure is formed inside of individual bacteria and is resistant to most adverse environmental factors such as temperature (heat

YOU NEVER KNOW WHERE YOU MIGHT FIND A RELATIVE

Imagine living in an environment so caustic and alkaline that warning signs would have to be posted to prevent you from coming in contact with any part of it. On the south side of Chicago, in the Lake Calumet region, live communities of microbes capable of dealing with a pH of 12.8. The closest known relatives of some of these microbes are in Mono Lake, California; Greenland; and South Africa.

The region in the Lake Calumet area was created when steel slag was used to fill in wetlands and lakes. Steel slag is a byproduct of steel production that contains calcium, magnesium, and aluminum in combination with silica. This created a region of contaminated materials that reacted with the water and air to form calcium hydroxide (lime), which drove up the pH to the extent mentioned.

Genetic analysis of the microbes at one site showed that the organisms were related to *Clostridium* and *Bacillus* species. Since *Clostridium* and *Bacillus* bacteria are routinely found in the soil, it seems plausible that the local bacteria adapted to this unique environment over the last 100 years. Another possibility is that the microbes were somehow imported into the region; however, this seems unlikely.

and cold), desiccation (dehydration), chemicals, radiation, pressure, extremes of pH, and common dyes (Figure 3.2).

Endospores differ from the vegetative cells that form them in a variety of ways. Several new surface layers develop outside the core (cell) wall, including the cortex and spore coat. The cytoplasm is dehydrated and contains only the cell **genome** and a few **ribosomes** and enzymes. The endospore is cryptobiotic (exhibits no signs of life) and is remarkably resistant to environmental stresses such as heat (boiling), acid, irradiation, chemicals, and disinfectants. Some endospores have remained dormant for 25 million years preserved in amber, only to be shaken back into life when extricated and introduced into a favorable environment.

Those bacteria capable of producing endospores begin the process, known as sporulation, when conditions are no longer favorable for growth (Figure 3.3). How bacteria are able to detect chemical changes in their environment continues to be the focus of much recent research.

Certain chemical substances appear to be required for sporulation. Included among them are glucose, which serves as an energy source; particular amino acids, which are needed as structural molecules; and growth factors including vitamins and minerals. Some of these growth factors may seem familiar since they are needed for our proper growth and development also. They include folic acid, phosphate, calcium, manganese, and bicarbonate, which serves as a buffer to maintain proper pH balance.

An endospore is not a reproductive cell. It functions more like a fallout shelter, serving as a survival structure. Only two genera of bacteria that produce endospores are currently of medical significance—the genus *Bacillus* and the genus *Clostridium*. There are other spore formers that are not known to cause human or animal diseases. These include *Sporosarcina*, the only coccal spore, which also happens to be a marine microorganism; *Sporolactobacillus*, found in chicken feed; and *Desulfomaculum*, an anaerobe, found in soil, water, and the intestines of some insects and cows.

Endospore

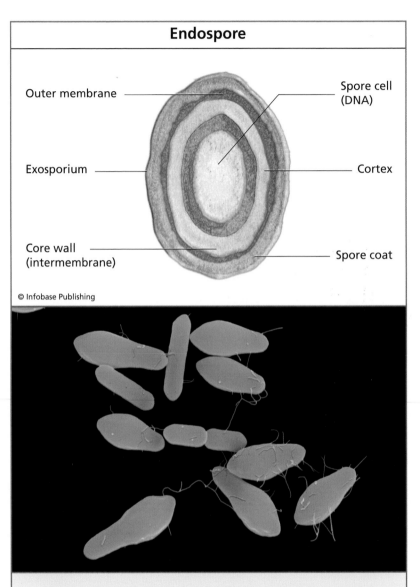

Outer membrane

Spore cell (DNA)

Exosporium

Cortex

Core wall (intermembrane)

Spore coat

© Infobase Publishing

Figure 3.2 The bottom image is a scanning electron micrograph of *Clostridium botulinum* cells. Note the swollen ends of some of the cells. This represents the position and shape of the endospore, which serves as a survival structure for the bacterium when conditions for its growth and survival become unfavorable. The top image illustrates the layers of an endospore (cross-section). (micrograph © Dennis Kunkel Microscopy, Inc./Visuals Unlimited, Inc.)

The ability to form endospores has made it possible for some species of bacteria to exist in a dormant state under unfavorable environmental conditions for long periods of time. This dormant state has provided these organisms the opportunity to survive under adverse conditions without being destroyed. In

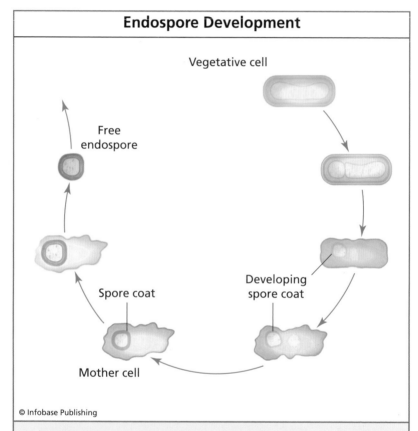

Endospore Development

Vegetative cell

Free endospore

Developing spore coat

Spore coat

Mother cell

© Infobase Publishing

Figure 3.3 The development of an endospore is illustrated here. When a bacterium senses that conditions have become unfavorable, it begins to develop the endospore. Using materials from the vegetative cell, it encloses its DNA, some RNA, and enzymes in a covering. This covering includes cell wall materials that have been impregnated with additional molecules that give the new structure incredible strength against environmental factors. The rest of the cell dies away, leaving the endospore to wait for favorable conditions that allow it to germinate back into the original cell.

HOW BACTERIAL CELLS COMMUNICATE

Biologists have long speculated that bacteria are able to communicate with each other and their environment by releasing and then detecting various types of chemicals. This activity is a form of molecular census taking and is usually called "quorum sensing." Evidence indicates more than 70 different types of organisms are engaged in this activity. Zhao (Zhao, et al., 2000) was the first to suggest that *Clostridium botulinum* also are involved in this quorum sensing. In a more recent article (Zhao, et al., 2003) in *Applied and Environmental Microbiology*, the original work was confirmed using a computer simulation program.

turn, their chance to be infectious for long periods of time is increased. Having the ability to form an endospore also makes bacteria impervious to many man-made chemicals designed to eliminate them from a variety of sources.

Types of Neurotoxins Formed

Clostridium botulinum is a genetically diverse species. Within the species, there are slight genetic differences that allow certain groups to produce different types of toxic proteins. There are seven distinct types of these toxins, each designated by a letter A through G. One reference source suggests an eighth toxin type designated as C_2. The clinical significance of C_2 is currently unknown. All of the toxins, except C_2, are considered neurotoxins, meaning that they affect the nervous system. Each of these toxins is a unique protein and can be used as a marker when trying to determine the cause of botulism poisoning. Other species have **strains** which can produce botulinum toxins. These species include *Clostridium baratii*, *Clostridium butyricum*, and *Clostridium argentinense*.

Type A toxin is considered the most lethal type. Types A, B, E, and occasionally F, cause human disease. Various domesticated animals, such as dogs, cattle, and birds of all types, are affected by type C. Type D has also been known to cause problems for cattle, while horses react to types A, B, and C. There are no known cases of animal or human botulism associated with type G toxin.

Types A, B, and F are capable of breaking down proteins and are therefore called **proteolytic**. When they break down proteins, there is often a foul odor in the food that may serve as a warning of bacterial contamination. These strains produce endospores that are very heat resistant. Non-proteolytic types, such as B, are able to grow in refrigerators and do not give off foul odors. Their spores are of low-heat resistance. According to recent studies and information published by NBC's Medical Information Server, the type A botulinum toxin is much more toxic than two other well known nerve agents—VX and Sarin (15,000 and 100,000 times more toxic, respectively). A dosage of only 0.001 micrograms of toxin type A per kilogram of body weight killed 50% of the animals tested. It has been suggested that a single gram (0.04 oz.) of the toxin in crystalline form, if inhaled, would kill more than one million people. The estimated human lethal dose is 0.01 micrograms per kilogram of body weight if the toxin is inhaled and 1.0 microgram per kilogram (2.2 lb) if taken orally.

This common soil organism has the capability of producing proteins that can sicken, paralyze, or kill vertebrate organisms, including humans. The most common protein to affect humans, type A, has most commonly caused food poisoning. Usually this poisoning has been unintentional. Unfortunately, there continues to be concern that rogue nations or terrorist groups might crystallize the type A toxin and use it as a weapon of mass destruction.

Recent work (2008) has provided a more complete description of how type A toxin attaches to its co-receptors on the nerve cell surface. This binding helps position the toxin for entrance into the nerve cell. This new information provides a greater understanding of the action of the botulinum neurotoxins. This new understanding could be applied toward the development of therapeutic agents which could block access of the toxin to the neuromuscular juntion or prevent the toxin from being taken into the digestive system.[1]

A collaboration between scientists at the U.S. Department of Energy's Brookhaven National Laboratory and the U.S. Army Medical Research Institute of Infectious Diseases (USAMRIID) has resulted in the development of a highly efficient inhibitor of botulinum neurotoxin type A. Type A is considered the most potent of the toxins. As mentioned earlier this represents a first step towards designing an effective antidote to the most potent form of the toxin. The scientists developed a technique which allowed them to block the actions of the toxin by tricking the toxin into ignoring its normal binding protein." This finding can lead to a very effective drug to stop the devastating effects of the toxin," said Brookhaven Lab biologist Subramanyam Swaminathan, the study's co-principal investigator. "We intend to do further research to tailor the inhibitor for the best results." The results of their research are reported in the April 22, 2008 online issue of the *Journal of Biological Chemistry*. This research was funded by the Defense Threat Reduction Agency of the U.S. Department of Defense. The NSLS is supported by the U.S. Department of Energy's Office of Basic Energy Sciences, Office of Science. [2]

Types A, B, E, and occasionally type F cause human disease. Various domesticated animals, such as dogs and cattle and birds of all types, are affected by type C. Type D has also been known to cause problems for cattle while horses react to types A, B, and C. There are no known cases of animal or human botulism associated with type G toxin.

Scientists at Brookhaven National Laboratory have determined the atomic-level structure of subtype E botulinum neurotoxin. The detailed structure was published online December 22, 2008, by the *Journal of Molecular Biology*.

The structure provided a surprise to the scientists who had expected a structure similar to the other toxin types. It has been suggested that this unique arrangement of the active components may explain why neurotoxin subtype E (one of seven distinct subtypes) is faster-acting than other subtypes previously studied at Brookhaven Lab. This unique structure may have implications for improving vaccines and/or therapeutic agents. "Understanding the differences among the seven botulinum neurotoxin subtypes is particularly imperative at a time of heightened concern about the potential use of these toxins as bioterror weapons," said Brookhaven biologist and lead author Subramanyam Swaminathan, who has conducted extensive research on botulinum neurotoxins supported by DOE, the U.S. Army, and the National Institutes of Health. Although experimental vaccines administered prior to exposure can inhibit the neurotoxin's destructive action, no effective pharmacological treatment exists. Finally, considering the threat of botulinum neurotoxin being used as a bioterror weapon, Swaminathan said, "The finding of a significant variation in the structural arrangement of subtype E also makes it clear that we must study the structures of the four remaining subtypes to gain a better understanding of their individual characteristics so that appropriate counter-measures can be developed for all seven forms."[3]

4

Transmission of Botulism

The Savannah River Bridge was just ahead. Once Jim crossed the river, he would be in Georgia and a little more than an hour's drive from his grandmother Emma's house. She was always kidding that she lived just south of paradise; it was her little joke about living south of the hamlet of Eden. During his last trip, he had visited the Ohoopee River Dunes area, a Nature Conservancy site unique to the state of Georgia. Jim had visited his grandmother with his parents and sister, Lindsay. He had been curious about the almost desert-like dunes and their threatened and endangered plants and animals in an inland area of Georgia.

Jim's current visit to his grandmother was meant to be a short stopover as he visited a number of universities in the area. Jim was beginning to look for places where he might attempt a master's degree. He was interested in looking at a number of universities along the East coast with master's programs in his area of healthcare administration. Armstrong Atlantic State University in Savannah, Georgia, had two master's programs that looked interesting. One was in Public Health, and the other was in Health Services Administration. Georgia Southern University in Statesboro, Georgia, also offered the same two degrees. Both were close to his grandmother and not far from the beaches.

Jim had visited Georgetown University in Washington, D.C. and George Mason University in Manassas, Virginia. Both had developed new master's degree programs in bioterrorism. The Georgetown program offers a Master of Science in Biohazardous Threat Agents and Emerging Infectious Diseases. The program has some interesting courses such as biosurveillance, microbiology of infectious agents, and chemical threat agents. The program is partnered with the Homeland Security

Institute, a division of a defense contractor known as Analytical Services (AS). It would be possible to be trained by AS and get a paid internship. As tempting as it sounded, Jim was fairly certain that he did not want the hustle and bustle of Washington, D.C.

George Mason University runs the Biodefense Degree Program. The Biodefense Graduate Program is affiliated with George Mason's National Center for Biodefense. Since its inception in 2002, the program has grown to more than 200 master's and doctoral students. The program was designed to teach more general principles in the areas of biotechnology, immunology, and drug discovery and development. There are four tracks in the program: medical defense, engineering defense, nonproliferation, and law enforcement/counterterrorism. Each of the four tracks is designed to provide graduates with a broad background and outlook that will increase the likelihood of employment in the area of biodefense in government, industry, or academic settings.

The sign for Jim's grandmother's town came into view. Fifteen minutes later, he arrived. Grandma Emma did not disappoint him. As soon as he got out of the car, she gave him a hug and kiss, commented on how big he had gotten, and offered him some iced tea and assorted pastries. The afternoon passed quickly, reminiscing about family and Jim's future plans. At dinner, Grandma Emma brought out Southern fried chicken, grits, and okra and tomato mixture. Dessert was ice cream and coffee.

After dinner, they sat out on the screened-in back porch watching the sun go down and listening to the small animals scampering about. Tomorrow, Jim would enjoy a potluck dinner with his grandmother and some of her friends.

POTLUCK DESTINY

Jim's grandmother baked an apple pie the next morning for the potluck. On the way to the dinner, they picked up her next-door neighbor, Mrs. O'Riley, who brought some of her home-canned beans. While Jim was driving, he listened to the conversation of the two women. Apparently, Mrs. O'Riley was originally going to bring some of her canned carrots, but didn't like their taste and so she brought the beans instead. It was still light when they arrived and everyone was milling around and chatting. All sorts of food were provided, including fried chicken, fish, macaroni and cheese, salads of all types, beans, squash, okra, collard greens, rice and baked potatoes with and without cheese, and even some sautéed onions. Desserts included pies; deep-dish peach, cherry, and apple cobblers; bread pudding; and fruit. Iced tea, soda, and coffee were served. Quite a buffet! Jim sampled a lot of food, but the fried chicken and cobblers especially caught his attention. He left feeling quite full.

After a wonderful night's sleep, Jim woke feeling refreshed but still quite full from the night before. He decided to take a jog and get some exercise. Later that afternoon, Jim decided to take a ride around the Savannah area and told his grandmother he would get something to eat in town.

When Jim returned to his grandmother's house later that evening, he noticed that her car was gone. It seems that his grandmother had taken Mrs. O'Riley to the local hospital. The answering machine contained a message from his grandmother with directions to the hospital.

Mrs. O'Riley had been brought into the emergency ward and seen by a local doctor who was on call. Her initial symptoms consisted of double and fuzzy vision, slurred speech, and dry mouth. After the doctor had finished speaking with Mrs. O'Riley, he sent her to one of the larger hospitals in Savannah for treatment. The doctor indicated he would like to talk to Grandma Emma and Jim about Mrs. O'Riley.

He explained that Mrs. O'Riley was very weak and ill, but he did not believe that she had had a stroke. He asked them for some information so that he could confirm his initial diagnosis. The doctor asked them to relate everything they were aware of

FOODS KNOWN TO BE ASSOCIATED WITH BOTULISM

Most of the outbreaks of foodborne botulism in the United States have been caused by improperly home-canned foods, mostly fish and low-acid vegetables (Figure 4.1). Included in this list of vegetables are string beans, corn, beets, spinach, asparagus, and chili peppers. Even plants in oil, such as garlic, chili peppers, and tomatoes, have been implicated. Sautéed onions and potatoes wrapped in aluminum foil have been known to contain endospores and cause botulism.

Fruits, such as figs, apricots, pears, peaches, applesauce, persimmons, and mangoes, also have been involved in some of these cases. If the canning process is done improperly or if food is left out after it is has been cooked initially, molds, yeasts, or bacteria may be allowed to grow. This may cause the pH of the food to be raised sufficiently to permit the growth of *C. botulinum*. In those under one year of age, honey is also an implicated food.

happening within the last three days, including what they ate and what was said about the taste or smell of any food. Jim's grandmother explained the potluck dinner and listed all of the foods that had been present. Jim mentioned the foods he had eaten and noted they all smelled and tasted great.

The doctor asked if Mrs. O'Riley had commented about the taste or smell of any of the foods. Jim's grandmother related that Mrs. O'Riley had tasted some of her canned carrots and decided not to bring them because they tasted bad. Mrs. O'Riley did not have a pressure cooker and used a boiling-water canner. Dr. Everett indicated that they had helped him confirm his diagnosis.

Figure 4.1 All sorts of foods can contain the botulism toxin. Shown are honey, which is implicated most frequently with infant botulism; onions that can carry endospores on their exterior surfaces; and canned foods that can harbor the anaerobic organism and its toxins if not properly heated during the canning process (© Petrenko Andriy/ Elena Rostunova/ Elena Elisseeva/ shutterstock images)

Jim was curious and asked what the doctor believed the problem to be. Dr. Everett's answer surprised Jim, saying "Mrs. O'Riley probably has botulism. We will need to get a sample of the canned carrots to help confirm the diagnosis clinically." Jim and his grandmother set up a time that lab technicians could visit the O'Riley house and check out the canned carrots.

Jim knew nothing about botulism. Other than knowing that it caused food intoxication and was caused by *Clostridium botulinum*, his knowledge was somewhat sparse. The doctor explained that he had seen a case very similar to Mrs. O'Riley's in Wisconsin in the early 1990s. The woman had sampled canned carrots and decided not to serve them to her guests because of the taste. The symptoms that had caused Dr. Everett to consider botulism had been the double vision, slightly slurred speech, and dry mouth along with the fact that Mrs. O'Riley was still mentally alert. These were all common signs of botulism intoxication. The fact that Mrs. O'Riley had also mentioned the bad-tasting carrots, a fact confirmed by Jim's grandmother, provided further evidence that her condition might be botulism. The doctor also indicated that it had taken more than six months for the woman in Wisconsin to recover, only after extensive physical therapy.

Mrs. O'Riley might have a long road to recovery in front of her. The doctor explained which hospital Mrs. O'Riley would be at and mentioned that he had to call the state health department and inform them of the presumed botulism case. The state health department would then report this information to the Center for Disease Control (CDC), who would then consult with the state health department over the phone and release the botulinum **antitoxin** used for treatment. The current regulations require that any case of botulism be reported so that it may be investigated and determined if it is part of a larger group outbreak that may be related to terrorist activity.

Jim followed his grandmother home and tried to console her. She asked if she should throw out all of her canned vegetables even though she had used a pressure cooker to do the canning. Jim suggested they look at the food and see if it looked spoiled. He also suggested that if it smelled bad when it was opened, it should not be tasted or eaten. His grandmother agreed.

DETECTING LIFE'S LITTLE SURPRISES IN OUR FOOD

Food contamination is not limited to beans and beef. In 2008, pistachio nuts were found to house *Salmonella*. In June 2009, the unthinkable occurred and Nestles' chocolate chip cookie dough was found to contain *E. coli O157:H7*, causing the hospitalization of at least 25 people, seven of those suffering with a severe type of kidney failure.

Finding the potential source of the contamination has become an exercise in molecular biology dependent upon high-quality extraction of the DNA, RNA, and proteins of the suspected pathogens. Unfortunately, some of the current extraction methods such as heat, electrical charge, and chemical separation can alter or destroy the very molecules that are being sought.

Happily, new extraction techniques are being developed that will allow a more accurate and efficient way to prepare samples for analysis. Dr. Edmund Ting, senior vice president of South Easton, Massachusetts–based Pressure BioSciences, Inc., cited the example of pressure cycling technology (PCT). This technique uses cycles of hydrostatic pressure to safely and efficiently release DNA, RNA, and proteins from food, plant, and biological samples within minutes. PCT technology is currently used by more than 75 laboratories worldwide including at least one FDA laboratory.

Food safety involves more than just the detection of bacteria but also dealing with chemicals released by these bacteria. In addition, we have added the challenge of dealing with genetically modified organisms (GMO) and their products. The new techniques will continue to improve the identification of these pathogens and their products. "Higher levels of quality are now being expected from the food industry and the scientific community to develop better ways to increase the safety of the world's food supply," says Ting.

The May/June 2009 issue of *Agricultural Research*, Volume 57, Number 5 contained an article entitled "Bashing Botulism: Scientists Sleuth World's Most Powerful Toxins" by Marcia Wood. While setting forth all of the normal warnings signs associated with food contaminated with *C. botulinum*, the article described research being done in Albany, California, to detect the botulinum toxin more quickly and efficiently. The work is being undertaken by scientists at the Foodborne Contaminants Research Unit, a section of the Agricultural Research Service Western Regional Research Center, which is part of the U.S. Department of Agriculture.

The new test uses molecules called *monoclonal antibodies*, which are laboratory-constructed proteins with a specificity for a particular type of protein, in this case botulinum toxin. While monoclonal antibodies of this type are not new, Dr. Larry Stanker and his colleagues have made these antibodies ten times more sensitive than the current mouse assay while being much less expensive.

This test, which also can determine if the toxin in the food sample is an active or inactive form, is relatively inexpensive and only takes about 20 minutes to perform.

5

Diagnosis of Botulism

Jim followed his grandmother home from the emergency room of the hospital. After pouring herself and Jim some iced tea, his grandmother found the telephone number of Mrs. O'Riley's daughter in Atlanta and called her. Next, Jim and his grandmother went to the storage area in the back pantry where grandmother kept all of her home-canned fruits and vegetables. Her first thought was to throw away all the home-canned foods even though she had used a pressure cooker in her canning and not a boiling-water canner like Mrs. O'Riley. Jim persuaded his grandmother that this would not be necessary and together they inspected all the canned foods. None appeared swollen or had any odor. Swollen cans and foul smells from canned materials would be one indication of contaminated food. After that inspection, Jim and his grandmother washed their hands carefully.

COLLECTING THE SAMPLES

Just before 4:00 P.M., the hospital van pulled up. Three technicians wearing white coats got out. Jim had visions of people in outfits similar to space suits; he was a little disappointed. He and his grandmother took the technicians into Mrs. O'Riley's house, and showed them where the home-canned materials were located. Without entering the pantry, the men made a quick observation, and two of them went back out to the van to get some additional materials. The third man suggested that Jim and his grandmother come outside with him while the other men went back inside to collect the samples.

One of the technicians explained what the other two men would be doing. All of the jars of vegetables and fruits would be collected for testing.

The jars would be placed in individual plastic bags, each of which must be labeled with the date and place of collection, the general condition of the jar, and suspected cause of the patient's illness. The jars would then be placed in leak-proof containers and quickly transported to the nearest public health lab. In this case, the samples were to be transported to the CDC in Atlanta. The samples would be kept cool, usually 2–8°C (35.6–46.4°F), and carefully packed to avoid the possibility of spillage. The receiving lab would be informed as to how the samples were being sent and their anticipated time of arrival.

The technicians must wear masks to prevent the possibility of contamination if one of the jars breaks and aerosolization occurs. Aerosolization is the process of creating very small particles that can be spread through the air. The two technicians who collected and transported the food had been immunized against the botulinum toxin. The personnel in Atlanta who would be testing the food had also been immunized against this toxin.

Closed containers of food suspected of being tainted with the botulinum toxin are among the easiest to package and transport. Other types of specimens require different collection and transport procedures. Table 5.1 illustrates some of the different methods that would be used.

It took the technicians about an hour and a half to finish the collection and packaging of the materials. A total of were 64 jars of home-canned vegetables and fruits that were finally collected.

HOW BOTULISM MAY BE DIAGNOSED

Botulism is not a common disease and is often underdiagnosed by doctors because they are not familiar with it, and the symptoms mimic many other diseases. In addition, the initial diagnosis of botulism is based on the patient's medical history given on admission to the hospital and the physical characteristics observed by the attending physician. Often diagnosis is made

Table 5.1 Collection and Transport of Laboratory Specimens for the Diagnosis of Botulism[1]

Specimen	Clinical	Collection and Transport
Serum	Intentional release, foodborne botulism, autopsy specimens Wound botulism (critical specimen for confirmation)	Collect whole blood; ship at 4°C (39.2°F); keep specimen refrigerated at all times Notify testing lab if patient has received stigmine drugs or a Tensilon test
Wound/tissue	Wound botulism	Collect discharge, tissue samples or swabs; ship at room temperature in airtight transport system
Stool, enema fluid, intestinal fluid	Intentional release, foodborne botulism, infant botulism, wound botulism†	Obtain 10-50 g (0.35-1.76 oz.) of stool (as little as "pea-size" for infant botulism); ship at 4°C (39.2°F); enema fluid can be collected; intestinal fluid at autopsy can be collected
Gastric fluid, vomitus	Intentional release, foodborne botulism, autopsy specimens	Collect within 72 hours of symptom onset; ship at 4°C (39.2°F); obtain sample of vomitus; obtain sample of gastric fluid (living cases or at autopsy)
Specimens to collect at autopsy	Intentional release, foodborne botulism, infant botulism	Serum, according to methods outlined above; contents from different sections of small and large intestines (10 g [0.35 oz.] per sample in separate containers); gastric contents and tissue samples as indicated, according to methods outlined above
Food samples (epidemiologically implicated)	Intentional release, foodborne botulism, infant botulism	Obtain 10-50 g of implicated or suspect food; ship at 4°C (39.2°F); place individually in leak-proof, sealed transport devices
Nasal swab	Intentional release‡	Obtain swab and transport in airtight container; ship at room temperature
Environmental sample	Intentional release, infant botulism	Collect as appropriate: environmental swab, soil (50-100 g [0.35-3.53 oz.]), Water (>100 mL [73.38 fl. oz.]); ship at room temperature

† A wound may not be the actual source of infection/intoxication.

‡ Toxin may be present on nasal mucosa for up to 24 hours after inhalational exposure (see bibliography: Franz 1997).

before the patient is tested for the presence of toxins or the culturing of bacteria. This is due to the need to begin treatment quickly, so that the patient can begin to recover.

The following summarizes the important methods recommended by the American College of Physicians when attempting to diagnose botulism:

- Use history to elicit neurologic symptoms and details of exposure compatible with botulinum toxin poisoning.

- Consider cranial nerve abnormalities as key findings in the diagnosis of botulinum toxin poisoning.

- Collect body fluid samples quickly to confirm the diagnosis of botulinum toxin poisoning.

- Schedule nerve conduction studies to confirm botulinum toxin poisoning but do not delay treatment to obtain this test.

- Perform other studies if the clinical picture is confusing.

- Consider other more common causes of bulbar weakness in the differential diagnosis of botulinum toxin poisoning.

Botulism is frequently misdiagnosed (Table 5.2), most often as Guillain-Barré Syndrome (GBS), stroke, or myasthenia gravis (MG). Guillain-Barré Syndrome, also called acute inflammatory demyelinating polyneuropathy and Landry's ascending paralysis, is an inflammatory disorder of the peripheral nerves—those outside the brain and spinal cord. It is characterized by the rapid onset of weakness and often, paralysis of the legs, arms, breathing muscles, and face. Myasthenia gravis is a disorder that results in easily fatigable muscle weakness, made worse by activity and improved with rest. It results from an autoimmune attack against the nerve-muscle junction. Other forms of the illness are caused by changes in the structure of the cells at the nerve-muscle junction. Muscles that control eye and eyelid movements, facial expression, chewing, talking, and swallowing are often, but not always, involved. The muscles that control breathing and neck and limb movements may also be affected.

Table 5.2 Differential Diagnosis of Botulism

Condition	Features
Guillain-Barré syndrome (GBS) (particularly Miller Fisher variant)	Usually an ascending paralysis, although Miller Fisher variant may be descending and may have pronounced cranial nerve involvement; abnormal CSF protein 1–6 weeks after illness onset (although may be normal early in clinical course); paresthesias commonly occur (often stocking/glove pattern); EMG shows abnormal nerve conduction velocity; facilitation with repetitive nerve stimulation does not occur (as with botulism); history of antecedent diarrheal illness (suggestive of Campylobacter infection)
Myasthenia gravis	Dramatic improvement with edrophonium chloride (although some botulism patients may exhibit partial improvement following administration of edrophonium chloride); EMG shows decrease in muscle action potentials with repetitive nerve stimulation
Tick paralysis	Ascending paralysis; paresthesias; careful examination reveals presence of tick attached to skin; recovery occurs within 24 hours after tick removal; EMG shows abnormal nerve conduction velocity and unresponsiveness to repetitive stimulation
Lambert-Eaton syndrome	Commonly associated with carcinoma (often oat cell carcinoma of lung); although EMG findings are similar to those in botulism, repetitive nerve stimulation shows much greater augmentation of muscle action potentials, particularly at 20–50 Hz; increased strength with sustained contraction; deep tendon reflexes often absent; ataxia may be present
Stroke or CNS mass lesion	Paralysis usually asymmetric; brain imaging (CT or MRI) usually abnormal; sensory deficits common; altered mental status may be present
Poliomyelitis	Febrile illness; CSF shows pleocytosis and increased protein; altered mental status may be present; paralysis often asymmetric
Paralytic shellfish poisoning or ingestion of puffer fish	History of shellfish (e.g., clams, mussels) or puffer fish ingestion within several hours before symptom onset; paresthesias of mouth, face, lips, extremities commonly occur
Belladonna toxicity	History of recent exposure to belladonna-like alkaloids; fever; tachycardia; altered mental status
Aminoglycoside toxicity	History of recent exposure to aminoglycoside antibiotics; more likely to occur in the setting of renal insufficiency; most commonly seen with neomycin; most commonly associated with other neuromuscular blocking agents such as succinylcholine and paralytics
Other toxicities (hypermagnesemia, organophosphates, nerve gas, carbon monoxide)	History of exposure to toxic agents: --Carbon monoxide toxicity: altered mental status may occur, cherry-colored skin --Hypermagnesemia: history of use of cathartics or antacids may be present, elevated serum magnesium level --Organophosphate toxicity: fever, excessive salivation, altered mental status, paresthesias, miosis
Other conditions	CNS infections (particularly brainstem infections); inflammatory myopathy; hypothyroidism; diabetic neuropathy; viral infections; streptococcal pharyngitis (pharyngeal erythema and sore throat can occur in botulism owing to dryness caused by parasympathetic cholinergic blockade)

Note: This differential diagnosis applies to botulism in adults and older children; infant botulism is not included since that condition is distinct from what would be expected during a bioterrorism attack.

Abbreviations: CSF—cerebrospinal fluid; EMG—electromyogram; CT—computed tomography; MRI— magnetic resonance imaging; CNS—central nervous system.

Because botulism may mimic other diseases, a number of other diagnostic tests may need to be performed. The results may seem confusing because the tests are attempting to both exclude other disorders as the cause of the symptoms and also include botulism as one of the contenders. By looking at the combined results of various tests, an assessment can be made more accurately about the possible cause of the symptoms.

Botulism differs from other conditions causing flaccid (not stiff) paralysis in that its primary effects are weakness and paralysis of the cranial nerves compared to milder muscle weakness below the neck, in its bilateral symmetry (on both sides), and in its absence of sensory nerve damage. Below are some other tests that are used in the diagnosis of botulism.

Computed Tomography Scan

The computed tomography scan (CT or CAT scan) uses a combination of X-rays and computer technology to provide pictures of all parts of the body in cross section. CAT scans can view the bones, brain, muscle fat, and organs. Brain imaging can be done very early in the presumptive diagnosis of the patient. Negative results, which really means that the scan is normal for the patient, may be part of a series of results that suggest the possibility of botulism. The CAT scan detects changes in the normal shape of organs, the presence of clots and visualize changes the in muscles of nerves. Changes in shape of organs or other changes in muscles or nerves would suggest diseases such as MG but not botulism.

Spinal Tap

During a spinal tap (also known as a lumbar puncture), fluid is removed from the spinal column and tested for any signs of infection (Figure 5.1). Like the CAT scan, a negative result with cerebrospinal fluid is suggestive of botulism. The fluid removed is the cerebrospinal fluid (CSF). CSF is normal in botulism and MG but protein levels in the fluid may be elevated with GBS. The spinal tap may be done within hours of the presentation of symptoms by the patient.

Spinal Tap

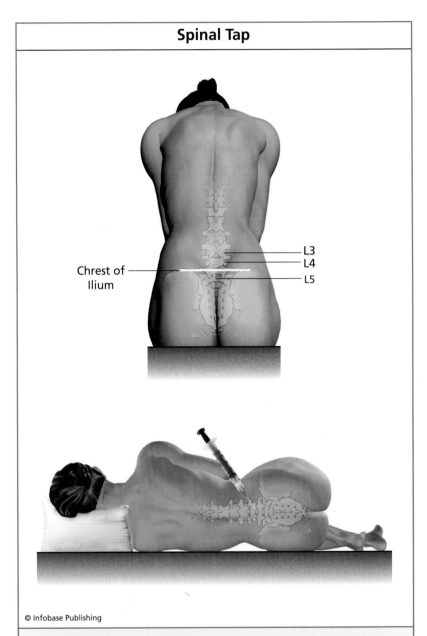

Chrest of
Ilium

L3
L4
L5

© Infobase Publishing

5.1 Removal of spinal fluid is accomplished by inserting a long needle into the spinal column in the lower or lumbar region in a procedure called a spinal tap or lumbar puncture. The fluid is examined for signs of infection.

Electromyogram

An electromyogram (EMG) measures the electrical activity of a muscle or a group of muscles. An EMG can detect abnormal electrical muscle activity. There are tests that will distinguish

BEATEN BY THE BEETS

A 70-year-old Oregon woman with a history of diabetes began to have double vision and dizziness. She visited her eye doctor who could find no obvious problem. Her daughter was having a sore throat, dry cough, and low-grade fever at the same time. She was admitted to the emergency room with double vision, given antibiotics for possible sinusitis (an infection of the sinuses), and sent home.

The next day, the daughter continued to feel poorly and her mother's health was also deteriorating. The mother was admitted to the hospital, followed by the daughter later that same afternoon. Having both mother and daughter with similar symptoms created concern among the hospital staff. The daughter mentioned they had eaten some nine-year-old, home-canned beets. In spite of that clue, the mother was diagnosed with a brain stem stroke and the daughter was thought to be experiencing some type of anxiety attack. Even though botulism was discussed, no one on the medical staff considered it a reasonable explanation.

The following day, the infection control nurse called the local health department to discuss the possibility of botulism. Botulism antitoxin was flown in from Seattle, Washington. Meanwhile, the mother had a heart attack and ultimately died. Laboratory data from the daughter showed that mice injected with fluid left over from the beets showed the characteristic signs of botulism, and then died. The daughter was treated and given supportive care. After a protracted recovery and physical therapy, she is now able to live a reasonably normal life.

botulism from myasthenia gravis. Most of them will result in a normal reading. The drug Tensilon is given, and then the patient does repetitive motion such as crossing and uncrossing of the legs to fatigue the muscles. If the drug improves the performance, the condition may be myasthenia gravis; if it does not improve, it could be botulism. A normal reading means that the performance of the muscle does not increase with the presence of the drug. The Tensilon test will be normal, as will the speed of the nerve conduction for GBS and botulism. With botulism, there will be a consistent increase in response to repetitive stimulation. However, a normal EMG does not rule out botulism, so this test must be used in conjunction with a good medical history and the other tests mentioned.

Mouse Test

The patient's **serum** or fecal matter (stool) is tested and cultured to detect the *Clostridium botulinum* organism. The patient's serum (the fluid portion of the blood with clotting factors removed) is injected into mice, and the subsequent symptoms are analyzed. The testing is done with mice because the serum contains the botulinum toxin and the amount may be too small to be detected by simple chemical testing. The mouse test is extremely sensitive and continues to be the gold standard against which all other tests are compared. It can detect as little as 0.03 ng of the toxin. A nanogram is a billionth of a gram. This botulinum toxin assay can be performed at the CDC and state public health laboratories. The mouse bioassay is the only diagnostic method currently used for detection and identification of botulinum toxin. The procedure requires that the patient's stool, serum, or other sample be injected into the abdominal cavity of the mouse (intraperitoneally). Other mice (called the "control" mice) receive a different sample—one containing both the sample to be tested and a neutralizing **antibody** against the various toxin types. Symptoms of botulism poisoning such as double vision, dry mouth, slurred speech and a paralysis that starts at the neck and works down, can occur within 6 to 24 hours.

Rapid, Non-Invasive Detection of Botulism

Currently, diagnosis of botulism requires that the patient's blood be drawn and then injected into a mouse. It takes at least 24 for the results. Certain toxins could cause paralysis or death within 18 hours. A new test can determine if an individual has been exposed to any of a number of toxins, including carbon monoxide, cyanide, organophosphate nerve agents, and botulinum. By measuring the pupil or retina of the eye a determination can be made in two minutes or less. The device is known as EyeMarker RTD 1000. The first trial results of the device correctly identified the presence or absence of botulinum toxin in the patients.

Michael S. Ascher, nationally known biodefense expert who coordinated the test trials in Alaska, indicated that "the findings are very dramatic and represent a clear proof-of-concept for the device in the diagnosis of exposure to botulinum toxin." Alaska was chosen because it has the highest number of cases of foodborne botulism in the United States.[2]

6

Botulism and the Nervous System

It has often been written that botulinum toxin is the most poisonous substance known. It is deadly at high concentrations and can be used therapeutically at low concentrations, such as for cosmetic procedures (see "The Positive Side of Botulinum Toxins"). One gram (.04 oz.) of crystalline botulinum toxin is sufficient to kill one million people. The toxin does its damage by blocking the release of an important chemical from the ends of the nerves in muscles. This prevents the muscle from receiving and responding to instructions in the form of a nerve impulse sent by the brain. It prevents a chemical, called acetylcholine, from being released from its storage structure and getting to the cell membrane by destroying the site where the chemical would bind. The toxin acts as an enzyme, which means it is not broken down or decomposed as a result of its action. It can carry out the same action over and over again. In other words, it is recyclable. This means that it only takes one or two toxin molecules to completely inactivate a nerve ending. To fully understand how this molecule carries out this activity, we will review the structures of the nervous system and their various functions.

THE NERVOUS SYSTEM

The nervous system is separated into two major divisions. The first division is made of the brain and spinal cord and is called the central nervous system (CNS). The second division is called the peripheral nervous system (PNS) and is made of nerves that carry messages to the CNS and a set of nerves that carry messages from the CNS to the muscles and glands. The two systems are interconnected and interactive (Figure 6.2).

THE POSITIVE SIDE OF BOTULINUM TOXINS

There are at least 50 different medical uses suggested for botulinum toxin. In recent years, the best known use has been to smooth out the wrinkles in aging skin. For the purposes of health insurance for patients over 12-years-old, the use of the toxins is considered to be either medically necessary, investigational, or cosmetic. Botulinum toxin is the first biological toxin to be approved as a medical treatment.

Examples of FDA approved diagnoses of medically necessary uses for botulinum toxin type A (Botox) include strabismus, also known as "lazy eye" or "crossed eyes." It was approved for this use in 1989. Overactive muscles are paralyzed with minute doses of botulinum toxin, allowing the remaining muscles to function properly, thus correcting the patient's vision.

A second muscle disorder of the eye is blepharospasm or eye twitching. This condition is significant historically because Canadian ophthalmologist Dr. Jean Carruthers noted the treatment's beneficial side effect of wrinkle reduction. The procedure involves injecting small amounts of botulinum toxin A into the offending muscle, which provides relief from twitching.

Some medical uses of FDA approved diagnosis for botulinum toxin type B (Myobloc) include cervical dystonia, a condition in which muscles in the neck and shoulders cramp severely. This usually causes the head to take unusual distracting positions. Injecting the toxin into the cramped muscles relieves the spasms. Botox was approved by the FDA for the treatment of cervical dystonia in December 2000.

Botulinum toxin type A and B injections are considered *investigational* for, but not limited to, a number of the following conditions: stuttering and other vocal tremors, chronic motor or tic disorder; (e.g., Tourette syndrome), and treatment of headache or migraine. Some patients experienced relief for up to six months when Botox was injected into muscles of the forehead, side of the head, back of the head near the neck, eye area, or brow area. Many patients who have strokes experience muscle spasms that cause clenching of hands and rigid muscles. Botox treatment is being used to relax those muscles so that stroke victims can gradually begin to reuse their hands and arms.

Although currently lacking FDA approval, Botox treatment of multiple-sclerosis-related symptoms is now considered an effective treatment option for certain types of problems. Botox injections have been shown in clinical trials to relieve spasticity in individual muscles for up to three months without any significant side effects.

The uses of botulinum toxin type A and B for the treatment of facial wrinkles are considered *cosmetic.* The FDA approved Botox for this purpose in April 2002.

Side effects have been mild in most instances and include symptoms such as, droopy eyelids, headaches, or nausea, in a small number of reported cases. In many instances, the results are short-lived and must be repeated every three months.

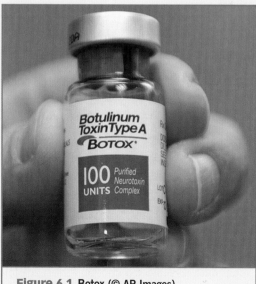

Figure 6.1 Botox (© AP Images).

The Nervous System

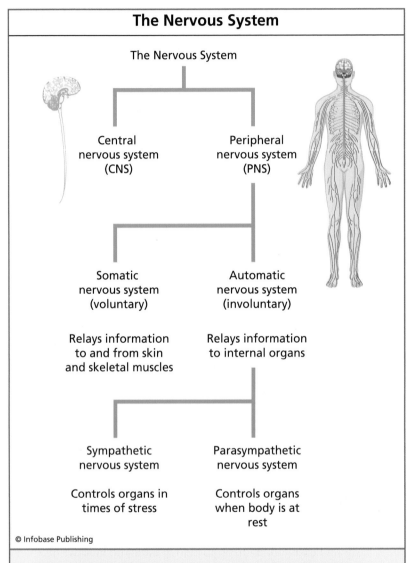

The Nervous System

Central nervous system (CNS)

Peripheral nervous system (PNS)

Somatic nervous system (voluntary)

Automatic nervous system (involuntary)

Relays information to and from skin and skeletal muscles

Relays information to internal organs

Sympathetic nervous system

Parasympathetic nervous system

Controls organs in times of stress

Controls organs when body is at rest

© Infobase Publishing

Figure 6.2 There are two major divisions of the nervous system. The central nervous system consists of the brain and spinal cord and sends messages, processes information, and determines the importance of that information. The peripheral nervous system consists of nerves that carry chemical messages to and from the central nervous system.

The central nervous system is often considered the control center of the body because it has multiple functions. The CNS does not have direct contact with the environment. Its job is to send messages, process information, and determine the importance of the information it is receiving. It is the job of the peripheral nervous system to relay this information from the environment to the CNS. The spinal cord serves as the communication link between the brain and the PNS.

The peripheral nervous system controls the areas outside the brain and spinal cord. The PNS can be subdivided into the sensory portion, which sends nerve impulses from the sense organs to the CNS, and the motor division, which sends nerve impulses from the CNS to the muscles or glands. The motor portion is also divided into two divisions, the somatic nervous system and the autonomic nervous system.

The somatic nervous system takes care of activities that are consciously controlled and usually involve the skeletal muscles. This system also contains many of the nerves that are part of reflexes that act automatically. The autonomic nervous system controls bodily functions that are not consciously controlled. The overall function of the autonomic nervous system is to maintain homeostatic balance in the functioning of the bodily organs and systems.

The autonomic nervous system is further divided into two parts that have opposite effects on the structures they regulate (Figure 6.3). The sympathetic portion of the autonomic nervous system usually speeds up action or activity and controls organs and systems when they are stressed by environmental factors. The parasympathetic portion of the autonomic nervous system regulates activity when the body is at rest and its action is normally to slow down the activity.

Cells of the Nervous System

Two types of cells make up nerve tissue. Cells that send nerve signals between the parts of the nervous system are the **neurons**

Sympathetic and Parasympathetic Nervous Systems

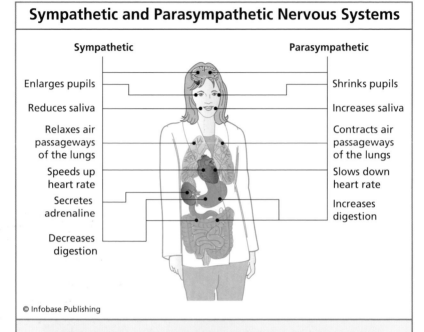

Sympathetic | Parasympathetic

Enlarges pupils — Shrinks pupils
Reduces saliva — Increases saliva
Relaxes air passageways of the lungs — Contracts air passageways of the lungs
Speeds up heart rate — Slows down heart rate
Secretes adrenaline — Increases digestion
Decreases digestion

© Infobase Publishing

Figure 6.3 The autonomic nervous system, which is further divided into the sympathetic and parasympathetic nervous systems, controls activities that are not under conscious control. The sympathetic portion controls organs and systems that are being stressed and usually speeds up activity. The parasympathetic portion controls the body when it is at rest (not stressed) and usually slows down activity.

(Figure 6.4). The second group of cells is the **neuroglia** or simply glial cells (Figure 6.5). Their function is to nourish and provide support for the neurons.

There are three different categories of neurons. A **sensory neuron** takes messages from a sensory receptor (a special structure that can sense environmental change) to the CNS. Next are the **interneurons**, which lie within the CNS. Interneurons receive impulses from sensory neurons and from other interneurons within the CNS. They compile the nerve impulses from the sensory neurons and interneurons before they contact the motor neurons. The **motor neurons** take nerve impulses from the CNS to an **effector**, a muscle or gland. Effectors are the final link in the chain that starts with the sensory receptors detecting the environmental change.

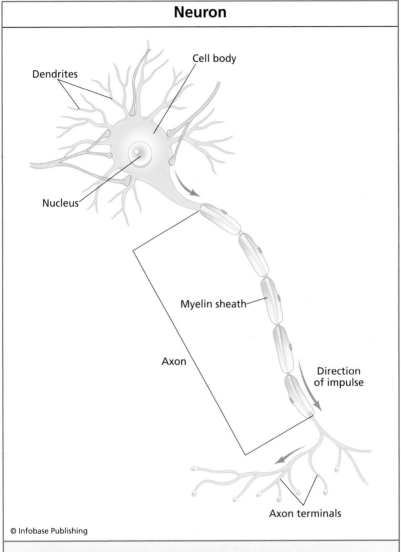

Figure 6.4 The neuron or nerve cell consists of a cell body or soma and two types of cellular extensions. A single long axon is normally covered by a fatty material, known as the myelin sheath. The axon transmits nerve impulses away from the cell body. Numerous dendrites carry nerve impulses to the cell body.

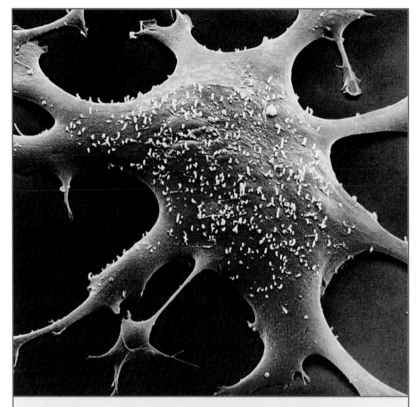

Figure 6.5 Shown here is a scanning electron micrograph of a glial cell, magnified 13,000 times. Glial cells provide nourishment and support for the neurons. (© Dr. David Phillips/Visuals Unlimited, Inc.)

How Things Work at the Cellular Level

When a nerve impulse passes along a nerve and reaches the junction of the nerve and muscle (neuromuscular junction), it causes the release of the chemical acetylcholine. This causes the muscle to contract. In order for this neurotransmitter, acetylcholine, to be released from the nerve cell, it must be brought to the cell membrane in an encapsulated form. This encapsulated structure is called a **synaptic vesicle**, and it must fuse or dock with the cell membrane in order to release the acetylcholine molecules. The merger of the vesicle with the nerve cell membrane is aided by a complex of proteins called the SNARE proteins (SNARE stands for Soluble NSF, or N-ethylmaleimide-sensitive fusion proteins). The three proteins are SNAP-25, synaptobrevin, and syntaxin (attachment protein receptor SNAP-25 stands for Synaptosomal-Associated Protein of 25 kilodaltons). This protein complex attaches the vesicle containing the acetylcholine molecules to the inside of the nerve cell membrane.

The synaptobrevin attaches to or "tags" the vesicle and then attaches to the SNAP-25–syntaxin complex that is already embedded in the bilipid layer of the nerve cell's membrane. Once bound to each other, the vesicle membrane merges with the cell membrane and turns inside out, releasing the acetylcholine into

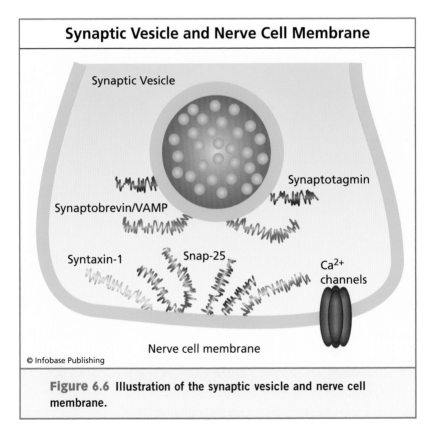

Synaptic Vesicle and Nerve Cell Membrane

Synaptic Vesicle

Synaptotagmin

Synaptobrevin/VAMP

Syntaxin-1   Snap-25 Ca^{2+} channels

Nerve cell membrane

© Infobase Publishing

Figure 6.6 Illustration of the synaptic vesicle and nerve cell membrane.

the space between the nerve and muscles cells. The acetylcholine attaches to receptors on the muscle cell membrane, resulting in contraction of the muscle.

THE BOTULINUM TOXIN MOLECULE

The botulism toxin molecule is produced by the *Clostridium* bacterium as a single large protein that is inactive. A protein is a large organic molecule made of carbon, hydrogen, oxygen, and nitrogen. A few proteins also contain sulfur. The structure, and thus the function, of a protein is genetically determined. Proteins are the end product of the genetic information. When the bacterium releases this protein, it comes into contact with enzymes that have been released by the bacterium or by the tissues of the body as part of their normal secretory activity. These enzymes break the large molecule into two unevenly sized pieces, or chains—a "heavy" chain and a "light" chain. The heavy chain is about twice as large as the light chain. The light chain is associated with an atom of zinc and this chain acts as a zinc endopeptidase, an enzyme with proteolytic action. An edopeptidase is a catalytic protein that breaks apart the peptide bonds that provide structural integrity to a protein. Thus the protein is broken apart and can no longer carry out its assigned function. It is the light chain that prevents the vesicle fusion. As mentioned earlier, the vesicle is an encapsulated structure. It can be thought of as a bag that contains chemicals, in this case acetylcholine. The vesicle is prevented from fusing with the cell membrane and releasing its chemicals.

The light chain of the toxin attaches to and chops up specific sites on the SNARE proteins. The type of toxin involved determines the specific protein that is chopped up. Types A, C, and E break up SNAP-25; types B, D, F, and G chop up synaptobrevin; and type C also chops up syntaxin. Since the vesicle cannot merge with the membrane, acetylcholine is not released and the muscle cannot contract. Because the major blocking mechanism is an enzyme, it can be used over and over again without destroying the toxin molecule itself.

Before and After Introduction of the Botulinum Toxin

The toxin is absorbed by the cells lining the stomach wall and intestines. The toxin passes into the bloodstream and diffuses into body tissues. The only portion of the body into which the toxin cannot spread is the central nervous system since the toxin molecule is too large to penetrate the blood-brain barrier. The toxin shape provides it a particular attraction to the membrane nerve endings of the peripheral nervous system. This temporary contact with a receptor on the nerve cell surface causes the nerve cell membrane to turn inward and surround the botulinum toxin. This engulfment process is called **receptor-mediated endocytosis** and brings the toxin molecule into the nerve cell. Once inside the cell, the toxin molecule interrupts the normal functioning of the SNARE protein complex. A portion of the toxin molecule called the light chain is released into the cell cytoplasm and breaks apart SNAP-25, a protein that is already part of the membrane of the nerve cell and is necessary for the release of acetylcholine. If SNAP-25 is broken apart, the vesicle containing the acetylcholine is not attached to the membrane and no message is sent to the muscle to contract.

Nerves Affected by Botulism Poisoning

In every case of botulism poisoning, the neurological signs show a characteristic pattern of equal and two-sided (bilateral) attack on the cranial nerves. A bilateral attack means that both sides of the body, on either side of the spinal column, are affected equally by the toxins. There are 12 pairs of cranial nerves that control the five senses. The head and neck are the initial starting point and the symptoms include difficulty in seeing with blurred and double vision, droopy eyelids, and problems with swallowing and speaking. The progression of the symptoms, including any paralysis, will vary with the patient and the amount of toxin consumed, as well as the toughness of the individual and his or her immune system. Because the brain is not attacked, the patient is still mentally alert but he or she is usually scared.

Botulism is not a common disease, so many clinicians have no first-hand experience with it. This can lead to mistaken diagnoses because the overt symptoms may suggest stroke, shellfish poisoning, tick paralysis, or conditions such as myasthenia gravis or Guillain-Barré syndrome. Whenever there are symptoms that involve the cranial nerves, botulism should be considered. If the patient has eaten home-canned foods or if there are others with the same symptoms who have eaten the same food, botulism should be considered. Because the nerves controlling the diaphragm can be attacked, the patient is at risk for respiratory distress and should be constantly monitored. It is critically important to begin treatment even before all the test results are in because once the toxin has attached to a nerve it will be a long time before that protein toxin will be broken down and can release that nerve, and that may be too late for the patient. Recovery usually involves the growth of new motor axon strands that attach to and reinnervate previously paralyzed muscle fibers. Unfortunately this a long process that usually takes weeks or even months to complete in adults.

7

Treating Botulism

Dr. Everett met Mrs. O'Riley's daughter in the lobby of the hospital. He had set up the meeting so he could prepare the daughter for some of the things she would see today and what the future treatment for her mother might be like. Dr. Everett particularly wanted her to understand why it was a good thing for her mother's bed to be in a head-up position (Figure 7.1). The greatest concern with botulism poisoning is the complication of breathing difficulties and possible respiratory failure. Treatment is designed to reduce the effects of the toxin, relieve symptoms, and prevent respiratory failure. The treatment received will depend on the severity of the symptoms. These symptoms may range from no change from normal to a rapid death within a day. If the symptoms become severe, hospitalization in an intensive care unit (ICU) is required.

BREATHING INTERVENTIONS

In the case of respiratory failure and the paralysis that usually occurs with severe botulism, a number of interventions may be required. One of these, **intubation**, requires that a tube be inserted through the nose or mouth into the **trachea** (windpipe) to provide an airway for oxygen. A second potential intervention is called **mechanical ventilation** where a machine is used to assist breathing. The proportion of patients with botulism who require mechanical ventilation ranges from 20 to 60%. These treatments help maintain an adequate oxygen supply. These interventions may be maintained for weeks or months, with additional intensive medical and nursing care for several months. If swallowing difficulties occur, the patient is given intravenous fluids and fed through a tube inserted in the nose. If all goes well, the paralysis will slowly improve over the next few weeks. Thanks to improvements in mechanical ventilation and intensive care, the **mortality rate** for foodborne botulism has dropped from 60% prior to 1950 to less than 15% currently. Some of those deaths are related to complications from using mechanical ventilation for more than two weeks. The most common are pneumonia and infection and damage to lung tissue from the movement of the tube.

SEEING THE WORLD FROM A DIFFERENT ANGLE

Mrs. O'Riley was not currently having severe breathing difficulties, so mechanical ventilation was not being used. If a patient is not severely impaired by the botulism toxin, a hospital bed placed in a reverse Trendelenburg position may postpone or avoid the need for mechanical ventilation. This position, which improves the positioning of the respiratory structures and provides protection for the airways, requires the patient to be placed on a flat mattress, which is tilted at 20 to 25 degrees. A tightly rolled cloth may be placed at the base of the neck to support the cervical vertebrae and similar items can be placed at the bottom of the bed to prevent the patient from sliding downward (Figure 7.1).

With treatment, most people recover completely from botulism-related paralysis. It may take several weeks or even months, and there may be lingering symptoms of shortness of breath and fatigue that may last for one year or more.

ELIMINATING THE TOXIN FROM THE BODY

A number of different methods are often attempted in an effort to eliminate the toxin from the body. Commonly, with foodborne botulism, the patient will have a procedure called **gastric lavage** where the stomach contents are pumped out to clear any toxin that has not yet been absorbed by the bloodstream. The patient might be given some medication to induce vomiting, or an enema or laxative to clean out the digestive tract. Treatment of food-related botulism exposures with non-magnesium-containing laxatives may further prevent absorption of the toxin. These techniques are most effective if the poisoned food has been ingested within the last few hours rather than more than a day.

While treatment for foodborne botulism has not changed in recent years, there is a new treatment for infant botulism. Called BabyBig or BIG-IV, the treatment is a solution made from human antibody proteins. This intravenous preparation will reduce the time that an infant will need to be in the hospital. Results of clinical

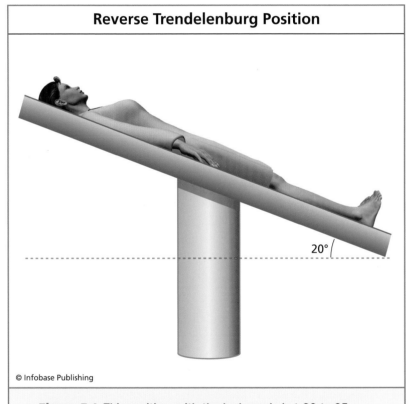

Reverse Trendelenburg Position

20°

© Infobase Publishing

Figure 7.1 This position, with the body angled at 20 to 25 degrees, helps to open up the airways, prevents nasal secretions from clogging the airways, and reduces the need for mechanical ventilation in mildly affected patients.

tests show a significant time reduction. The preparation can only be obtained from a particular source.[1]

Wound botulism is usually treated by surgically removing the skin of the affected area, a process called **debriding**. An **antibiotic**, such as Penicillin G, is recommended in the treatment of wound botulism. The role of antibiotics in the treatment of other types of botulism remains unclear except for the treatment of secondary infections complicating botulism. Certain antibiotics, such as the group known as the aminoglycosides and clindamycin, would not be used because they tend to cause the very type of nerve problems that need to be cured. Aminoglycosides do not work against anaerobic organisms such as *Clostridium*.

Antitoxin Therapy

An **antitoxin** is a type of antibody whose job is to neutralize toxins. It does not reverse the disease process, however. If botulism is detected and diagnosed early enough in the course of the disease, an antitoxin can stop the paralysis from progressing and may alleviate symptoms.

Because the antitoxin treatment for botulism is made from horse serum, which may contain some proteins the body regards as foreign, some patients may have an allergic response to the antitoxin serum. The attending doctor should be made aware whether the patient is sensitive to horse serum, so he or she may receive allergy medication prior to antitoxin treatment. If a patient does not know whether he or she is sensitive to horse serum, the doctor will inject a small amount and wait for 20 minutes to see if a reaction occurs, such as a rash at the injection site, a swelling at the lymph nodes closest to the injection site, or **shock**. Confirmation of botulism may take several days, and antitoxin is most effective if given within 24 hours after symptom onset. Antitoxin is normally given before the laboratory test results are known.

The antitoxin can be given for either foodborne or wound botulism and is designed to interfere with the action of the toxin, thus preventing further damage to the nerves. It is only effective if used early in the illness when the toxin is still in the blood and has not yet become attached to the nerves. (This must be done with care due to the risk of **anaphylaxis**, a severe form of allergic reaction which occurs in 10–20% percent of patients.) The antitoxin can stop the patient from getting any worse, but recovery still takes many weeks.

Antitoxin treatment is not generally used in cases of infant botulism. The immune systems of infants are immature and inexperienced and may thus develop a severe allergic reaction to horse serum. Therefore, they cannot receive the antitoxin used for adults. Respiratory help is the major treatment method for infants. This requires hospitalization, sometimes in the intensive care unit.

Problems Associated with Antitoxin Therapy

The antitoxin used for botulism is only available through the Centers for Disease Control and Prevention (CDC) by way of state and local health departments. California and Alaska are exceptions because antitoxin release is controlled by their state health departments. Case workers at the CDC are available 24 hours a day to provide advice regarding use of antitoxin. Resources are also available at the state level. Antitoxin is maintained at quarantine stations located in airports in various metropolitan areas (e.g., New York, Chicago, Atlanta, Miami, Los Angeles, San Francisco, Seattle, and Honolulu). Once antitoxin is requested for a patient with suspected botulism, it generally can be delivered within 12 hours. A pentavalent (ABCDE) botulinum toxoid is available through the CDC as an investigational new drug (IND). A toxoid is a chemically weakened toxin that can be used as a vaccine. A pentavalent toxoid means that five different toxins have been used to make the vaccine. This antitoxin is effective against toxin types A–E. However, it can only inactivate the botulinum toxin that has not yet attached itself to nerve endings. The sooner a victim

RED, HOT, AND ITCHY

Urticaria, which is also known as nettle rash or hives, is a type of skin eruption. In the simplest form, this translates as an itching with rash. The origin of urticaria is an allergic reaction. Characteristically the skin eruptions are red, circular, itchy, and slightly raised above the skin level. This red, raised characteristic is sometimes called a wheal or erythema. The itching is usually intense and becomes worse the more you scratch. The area will have a slight local warmth as the itching brings more blood into the area.

These eruptions can remain on the body for a variable period, anywhere between a few seconds to hours. They have a tendency to disappear and reappear. When they disappear, they do so without leaving behind any trace.

receives the antitoxin, the more the nerve endings may be preserved. The U. S. Army has developed an investigational heptavalent botulinum antitoxin (types A, B, C, D, E, F, and G). This product could potentially be used during a bioterrorist attack involving airborne forms of botulism. It is not currently known how well it would work with humans. Since 4% of the horse **antigens** remain in the preparation, there is a risk of hypersensitivity. The circulating equine (horse) antitoxins have a half-life of five to eight days. A half-life of an antitoxin is the amount of time required for one half of the antitoxin molecules to break down and lose their activity.

There are a number of common side effects from the antitoxin. They include **urticaria**, serum sickness, mild hypersensitivity, and anaphylaxis. Before any antitoxin is administered, the patient should be tested to determine whether he or she is sensitive to the antitoxin. Skin testing through a method called a scratch test is the most effective. With the scratch method, the skin of the arm or back is scratched with a sample of the proteins found in the antitoxin preparation (Figure 7.2). A positive test will show a red, raised area that indicates a sensitivity to the proteins and, thus, to the antitoxin preparation. Fortunately if the scratch test is positive, the patient can be desensitized using incremental doses of antitoxin administered over three to four hours.

Individuals whose immune systems are already primed to react to specific proteins are said to be sensitive to those proteins. Re-exposure of these individuals to the same proteins may cause an exaggerated (hypersensitive) or misdirected immune response that results in local tissue injury or in system-wide problems, including shock or death. In these cases, the immune response is disproportionate to the challenge. Immune responses that result in tissue injury or

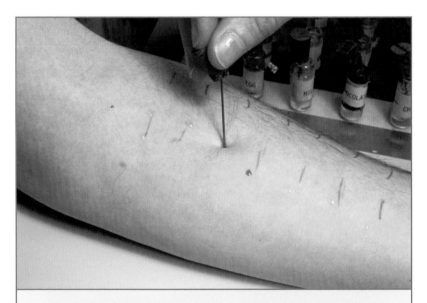

Figure 7.2 With the scratch test, a small amount of the material to be tested for allergy is placed on the skin (usually the forearm, upper arm, or the back), and then scratched or pricked into the skin so that the material gets under the skin surface. The skin is checked for signs of a reaction, which usually includes redness and swelling at the site. (© SIU/Visuals Unlimited, Inc.)

Table 7.1 Four Stages of Clinical Studies

Phase I
• 30 to 100 healthy volunteers.
• Small doses of the drug are given under highly controlled conditions in specialized clinics.
• Broad safety issues are studied before testing the drug with patients who have the disease or condition.

Phase II
• 50 to 300 patients who have the disease or condition.
• Studies if the drug has some effect against the disease, the drug's side effects, and the most promising dose and dosing regimen.

Phase III
• Tests an average of 3,000 patients, but can test as many as 10,000 patients.
• Tests are designed to establish the safety and effectiveness of the drug in a large and diverse population.

Phase IV
• Post-marketing studies to determine the drug's risks, benefits, and optimal use.

other pathophysiological changes are called **hypersensitivity** (allergic/immunopathological) **reactions**. Serum sickness is a hypersensitivity reaction similar to an allergy. The immune system misidentifies a protein in the antitoxin preparation as a potentially harmful molecule and develops an immune response against the proteins in the antitoxin preparation. Symptoms may not appear for as long as 21 days after exposure to the proteins. The time may be reduced to one to three days if patients have previously been exposed to the molecule. In a study conducted between 1967 and 1977, one series of 268 patients who received antitoxin, 24 (9%) had acute (13 patients) or delayed (11 patients) hypersensitivity reactions. The current recommended dose is less than that received by many patients in the study; therefore, the rate of hypersensitivity reactions occurring currently is likely to be somewhat lower than the reported rate.

The most dramatic result of severe hypersensitivity is anaphylatic shock or anaphylaxis. Anaphylaxis is a sudden, severe, potentially fatal, system-wide allergic reaction that can involve various areas of the body (such as the skin, respiratory tract, gastrointestinal tract, and cardiovascular system). Symptoms occur within minutes to two hours after contact with the allergy-causing substance, but in rare instances may occur up to four hours later. Most reactions occur within 30 minutes or less. Anaphylaxis is often called immediate-type hypersensitivity. The potential for these problems is the reason that patients are tested with small amounts of the antitoxin before they are given the full therapeutic amount. If they are sensitive to any component of the antitoxin they can be desensitized within a few hours, thus enabling them to safely receive the antitoxin.

CLINICAL STUDIES: TESTING NEW MEDICINES

One major weapon in the fight to treat certain bacterial and viral diseases is the use of **clinical trials** to determine if new drugs can be used safely and effectively on human volunteers.

Table 7.2 Vaccine Development for Botulism

Candidate	Development	Status
Heptavalent equine antitoxin (A–G)	Department of Defense (DOD	Investigational new drug (IND)
Polyvalent (A, B, E) equine antitoxin	Centers for Disease Control and Prevention (CDC)	FDA licensedClinical trials (for infant botulism)
Human botulism immune globulin (BIG) (A & B)	California Department of Health	Preclinical—very potent in mice
Recombinant antitoxin	University of California, San Francisco	Preclinical—very potent in mice Clinical trials—in about 6–9 months

The Food and Drug Administration (FDA) relies on these trials to determine the safety of the new drugs and the most effective way to use them to treat patients.

A new product is not tested on human volunteers until it has been shown to be safe in the laboratory and in animals. The testing protocols involve four phases that have been approved by the FDA (Table 7.1). A health care team monitors the volunteers' health from the outset of the trials to their conclusion.

Finding an effective treatment for botulism is a tricky business since there are seven types of botulinum toxin, designated from A through G. Antitoxins against one type of toxin do not neutralize the other types. There are a number of **vaccines** that are currently in some stage of the trial sequence (Table 7.2). The U.S. Army has developed a vaccine that has been shown to be safe in animals and human volunteers, but it is effective only for the A–E types. The vaccine status is known as investigational new drug (IND) status and it is not feasible to test for effectiveness in humans. After one year, this vaccine stimulates protective antitoxin levels in greater than 90% of those vaccinated. The vaccine should be used cautiously since there is a limited supply.

The most serious complication of botulism is respiratory failure. The aim of treatment is to maintain a constant supply of oxygen to the lungs. For some patients this may require a ventilator and close monitoring in an intensive care unit. Feeding through a tube may also be necessary. If treatment begins early, an antitoxin can stop the paralysis from progressing and may shorten symptoms. It does not reverse the disease process. Persons who will require long-term care may also require physical therapy to overcome the effects of the paralysis. Therapy for botulism consists of supportive care and immunization with horse antitoxin antibody. There are no other treatments that are currently licensed for use. Part of the supportive treatment may utilize the reverse Trendelenburg bed position but antibiotics do not work against toxins and thus are not used. If the intake of toxins is known to be recent, activated charcoal may be given to absorb the toxins before they enter the bloodstream.

On May 29, 2008, the Canadian pharmaceutical company Cangene made a large delivery of botulism antitoxin (BAT) to the U.S. government. This supply of antitoxin will be incorporated into the U.S. Strategic National Stockpile. According to the report, Cangene's BAT contains antibodies against all seven types of botulinum toxin.[2]

In April 2009, Cambridge Biostability and DynPort Vaccine Company announced the successful production of a thermally stable, rapidly injectable, pentavalent recombinant botulinum vaccine candidate. Their vaccine candidate is designed to provide protection against exposure to botulinum neurotoxin serotypes A, B, C, E and F.

8

Preventing Botulism

EDUCATING THE PUBLIC

In order to prevent botulism, it is necessary to educate the public. Based on data compiled by the CDC and reported in the *Morbidity and Mortality Weekly Reports* (MMWR), there were 632 total confirmed cases of botulism between the years 2000 and 2004. Of the 632, 126 or about 20% were designated as foodborne, 402 or about 64% were classified as infant botulism, and the remaining 16% were designated other, with most of those cases being associated with heroin users. The main form of human botulism throughout the world is the classic foodborne intoxication. While infant botulism remains rare throughout the world, it has become the most frequent form of the disease in the United States in recent years.

In the United States, there is an ongoing attempt to educate the public about the dangers of botulism and how to prevent it. Many resources exist that describe methods for safe canning. The CDC and the state health departments maintain a 24-hour hotline for physicians staffed with persons who are knowledgeable about botulism and available for consultation. Through this network, physicians who need antitoxin for patient treatment can have it delivered anywhere in the country. Physicians should report suspected cases of botulism to their state health department, as Dr. Everett did in the case of Mrs. O'Riley. If it is suspected that a case might represent an outbreak of botulism involving a commercial product, the public health and regulatory agencies will coordinate their efforts to bring a swift conclusion to the matter. State health departments and the CDC have persons knowledgeable about botulism available to consult with physicians 24 hours a day. Physicians report suspected cases of botulism to a state health department. If antitoxin is needed to treat a patient, it can be quickly delivered to a physician anywhere in the country. Suspected outbreaks of botulism are quickly investigated by the local health department and the CDC. The appropriate control measures are coordinated among public health and regulatory agencies.

In Europe, the public has become more aware of the risk of all types of food poisoning, including botulism. One exception has been Poland where foodborne botulism continues to be a serious health concern. This is due to the continuing practice in some parts of Poland of home-preserving meat and, to a lesser extent, vegetable and fruit products. In the 1960s, the 1970s, and during the turbulent times of social unrest and change during the 1980s, the incidence of botulism was high due to food shortages, causing people to use their home preserves.

FOODBORNE BOTULISM

While foodborne botulism represents less than 25% of the total cases in the United States, it is the segment that is written about the most. It is interesting that in order for *Clostridium botulinum* to cause an illness, a number of environmental factors all have to be met. An anaerobic environment would be necessary for the organism to germinate out of its endospore and produce its toxins. A low pH, between 4.6 and 7, is also necessary. This is a range of pH from mild acidity to neutrality. There must be an absence of preservatives, a large amount of moisture, and air temperature that is moderate (between 65–75°F [18.33–23.89°C]). These conditions rarely occur in foods (Figure 8.1).

During 1990 to 2000, the public became more interested in their health and began to look at the chemicals in food. Preservative-free, low-salt, commercially produced foods packaged in airtight containers became popular. Unfortunately, these conditions provided no detriment to the ubiquitous endospores of *C. botulinum*, which germinated in the anaerobic environment presented by the airtight containers. Like a seed, the term *germinate* refers to an opening up of internal material to the

Temperature and Bacterial Growth

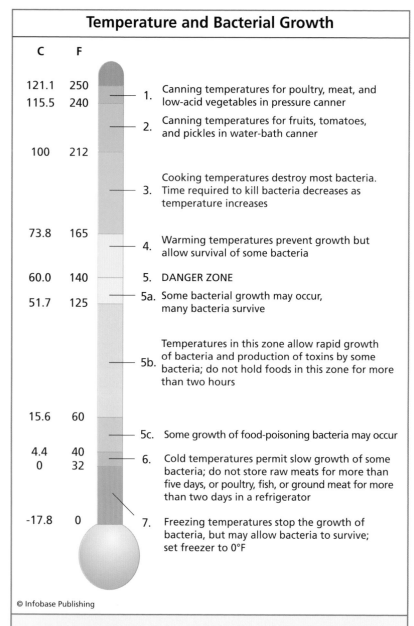

C	F	
121.1	250	1. Canning temperatures for poultry, meat, and low-acid vegetables in pressure canner
115.5	240	
		2. Canning temperatures for fruits, tomatoes, and pickles in water-bath canner
100	212	
		3. Cooking temperatures destroy most bacteria. Time required to kill bacteria decreases as temperature increases
73.8	165	4. Warming temperatures prevent growth but allow survival of some bacteria
60.0	140	5. DANGER ZONE
51.7	125	5a. Some bacterial growth may occur, many bacteria survive
		5b. Temperatures in this zone allow rapid growth of bacteria and production of toxins by some bacteria; do not hold foods in this zone for more than two hours
15.6	60	
		5c. Some growth of food-poisoning bacteria may occur
4.4	40	6. Cold temperatures permit slow growth of some bacteria; do not store raw meats for more than five days, or poultry, fish, or ground meat for more than two days in a refrigerator
0	32	
-17.8	0	7. Freezing temperatures stop the growth of bacteria, but may allow bacteria to survive; set freezer to 0°F

© Infobase Publishing

Figure 8.1 This thermometer shows both Celsius and Fahrenheit temperatures. Area 5 is the danger zone for the growth of bacteria. Above and below this zone, the reproduction rate drops off and eventually ceases.

outside environment. The bacterial cell that entered into the endospore stage during unfavorable conditions now leaves the newly opened endospore. That meant that the only way to slow or prevent the germination of the spores was through refrigeration. A temperature below 4° Celsius (about 39.2° Fahrenheit) will usually prevent the germination of the endospore. As the outbreaks associated with a commercial bean dip and clam chowder showed, this method did not prevent the germination of the organism or the production of the botulinum toxins. The only way to increase the efficiency of the airtight packaging and refrigeration was to add additional safeguards in the form of acidification and reduction of water content.

From 1990 to 2000 home-canned foods remained a leading cause of foodborne botulism in the United States. Botulism associated with Alaska native foods continues to be a problem because the use of glass and plastic for the fermentation of their blubber and fish has altered traditional practices and created an unsafe condition. Glass and plastic containers allow for the creation of an anaerobic environment favorable for growth of the botulinum organisms. The Alaska State Department of Health and Social Services, in partnership with the CDC, has developed culturally appropriate educational materials on safer native food preparation. The traditional method of fermentation involved digging a hole in the ground and covering the blubber with grass and dirt and allowing it to ferment in this environment. This creates a predigested mass of highly acidic food which is then consumed. The new method focuses on handwashing (which eliminates soil containing endospores); using safer, traditional fermentation processes; avoiding plastic and glass containers; boiling native foods before consumption to reduce the possibliity of bacterial contamination from soil; and discarding suspicious foods.

The World Health Organization (WHO) Fact Sheet No. 270, entitled *Botulism,* (revised August 2002) suggests that prevention of botulism is based on good food preparation (particularly preservation) practices and hygiene. Botulism may be prevented by inactivation of the bacterial spores in heat-sterilized, canned products or by inhibiting growth in all other products. Commercial heat pasteurization (vacuum packed pasteurized products, hot smoked products) may not be sufficient to kill all spores and therefore safety of these products must be based on preventing growth and toxin production. Refrigeration temperatures combined with salt content and/or acidic conditions will prevent the growth or formation of toxin.

Food safety requires a modern production and processing capability with quality control measures used to prevent the entrance of soil which may contain organisms or their endospores. Storage of food that has been properly prepared is enhanced by cold temperatures, a high degree of acidity in the food, or a high salt concentration which would inhibit the growth of soil organisms such as *C. botulinum*.

FOOD CANNING

Part of the reason that the Poles have such a high botulism rate is the fact that people often use a system of weck jars (weckglas) to hermetically seal cooked food at home. Weck jars are glass jars with rubber seals and a device used to create a vacuum. The two major problems with this technique are inadequate heating during the preparation of food and failure to follow detailed instructions during wecking, which leave spores viable and permits toxin formation. Destruction of spores requires a temperature of boiling or above for at least 24 hours and the wecking process does not accomplish this.

Boiling Water vs. Pressure Cooking

Two methods are used when doing home canning the boiling-water-bath method and the pressure canner or pressure cooker procedure. In both procedures, foods are heated in containers to temperatures that should destroy the microorganisms and their endospores, if any, that may otherwise cause sickness or spoilage of the food. The method chosen

Table 8.1 High-acid and Low-acid Foods*

High-acid Foods	Low-acid Foods
Apples	Asparagus
Applesauce	Beans, shelled
Apricots	Beans, snap
Berries	Beets
Cherries	Carrots
Cucumbers	Corn
Fruit juices	Hominy
Peaches	Mushrooms
Pears	Okra
Pickled beets	Peas
Plums	Potatoes
Rhubarb	Pumpkins
Tomatoes	Spinach and greens
Tomato juice	Squash

* Process high-acid foods in a boiling-water-bath canner and low-acid foods in a pressure canner, according to current methods.

usually depends on the type of food that will be canned. The boiling-water-bath method is normally used to can foods that have a very low pH, otherwise known as high-acid foods such as tomatoes, fruits, pickles, or sauerkraut. Table 8.1 uses the terminology of high-acid and low-acid foods. A low-acid food has a pH that is closer to 7, which is considered neutral. With the boiling-water-bath method, jars of food are completely covered with boiling water and heated for a specific period of time. A rough guide is about 5 to 10 minutes for pickles; 10 minutes for jam; about 20 to 30 minutes for fruit, fruit pie fillings, and applesauce; and 30 to 45 minutes or more for tomatoes. (Begin timing after the water begins to boil.) The time depends on the food, and the state or county extension agencies can provide information about the time necessary to heat each type of food.

When a pressure canner is used, the jars of food are heated under pressure to temperatures in excess of 240°F (115.56°C). This is a temperature above boiling and is necessary to destroy the endospores of *C. botulinum*. Low-acid foods can be safely canned using this method. Carrots are low-acid foods, so Mrs. O'Riley should have used a pressure cooker to do her carrot canning. Because she used a boiling-water canning method, the spores survived, and when they germinated, they produced their deadly toxins. As she found out, even a taste of food containing these toxins can be potentially fatal.

The major factor that determines whether food will be processed using a pressure cooker or the boiling-water bath is the acidity of the food. Pickled foods and most fruits have a pH that is acidic enough (below pH 4.6) to prevent the growth of the vegetative cells of *C. botulinum*. In most of the cases of commercial or residential canning that have led to botulism, the pH of the materials involved was 5 or higher.

INFANT BOTULISM

Although infant botulism cases represent nearly two-thirds of the total botulism cases in the United States, there is relatively little information about the mechanism of transmission and, thus, not much that can be said about prevention. Only about 5% of infant botulism patients apparently contract the disease from honey. Still, health officials and pediatricians agree honey should not be fed to infants less than one year of age. Honey is perfectly safe for older children and adults. They can eat the botulism spores found in honey without incidence, as intestinal bacteria and the immune system will kill off the spores.

Spores enter the infant intestine in the form of some contaminated food. After an incubation period of about one month, the spores then colonize in the intestines and produce toxins. Often it is not clear how the baby contracted the disease. Endospores of *Clostridium botulinum* are capable of existing in the soil and even the dust of a vacuum cleaner. It has also been shown that two other species of *Clostridium* can produce similar symptoms. While vaccination would seem to be an alternative, vaccines against infant botulism do not exist. Infant botulism is difficult to prevent because monitoring what goes into an infant's mouth is often beyond control, especially in regard to spores in the air. Food safety is the surest prevention for botulism. Never feed honey to infants younger than 12 months since it is one known source of botulism spores. As infants begin eating solid foods, the same food precautions should be followed as for adults.

WOUND BOTULISM

Wound botulism occurs when a toxin from *C. botulinum* infects a wound. A potentially lethal paralysis is the result. The wound can only become infected if the bacterium is introduced into an anaerobic pocket of the skin, such as occurs when deep cuts or wounds occur in muscle tissue in the arms or legs causing loss of blood flow and the oxygen carried by that blood. Only then will the toxins be produced and released. This form of botulism is normally associated with severe traumatic injuries of the extremities. In 1982, the first wound botulism case associated with drug use was reported in New York City. Between 1988 and 1995, 49 cases were reported of which 46 were drug users injecting black tar heroin (BTH). Of these 49 cases, only two cases (in Arizona) were outside of California. There appears to be a link between black tar heroin use and the contraction of wound botulism. According to Douglas Passaro, a professor of epidemiology and infectious diseases at the University of Illinois and special assistant for bioterrorism surveillance and epidemiologic response to the Illinois Department of Public Health, "Injection of BTH intramuscularly or subcutaneously is the primary risk factor for the development of [wound botulism]." The obvious preventative measures for wound botulism related to drug use would be to stop using the drugs.

COMMON SENSE, SAFETY, AND THE OBVIOUS

Preventing botulism requires educating the public. Unfortunately, a significant number of consumers are not up-to-date on proper handling and storage of foods. In a widely quoted 1992 study, it was found that consumers under 35 years of age knew less about food-safety terms and concepts than those over 35. Specific safe-food handling was not practiced by 15% to 30% of survey respondents. The need for sanitation was not recognized, with only 54% indicating they would wash a cutting board with soap and water between cutting raw meat and chopping vegetables. Respondents did not realize that food particles with bacteria attached could become caught in the crevices and be transmitted to other food that was processed

Table 8.2 Botulism Prevention Precautions

- Discard all raw or canned food that shows any sign of being spoiled.

- Discard all bulging or swollen cans of food and food from glass jars with bulging lids.

- Do not taste food from swollen containers or food that is foamy or has a bad odor.

- Can low-acid food in a pressure canner (to reach temperatures above boiling) for the recommended time, depending on the size of can or jar you are using.

- Do not can low-acid foods in the oven, in a water-bath, open kettle or vegetable cooker.

- Before eating home-canned low-acid foods, heat to a roiling boil, then cover and boil corn, spinach, and meats for 20 minutes and all other home-canned low-acid food for 10 minutes before tasting.

- When in doubt, throw it out.

on the same board. Since that time, the public has become more aware of potential problems.

Among the factors that have contributed to a lack of consumer understanding regarding food safety and storage have been few home economics courses required in high school and people eating out more frequently. Ironically, eating out increases the possibility of exposure to botulism. Most of the people preparing and serving your meals are the same people who are not aware of the problems of bacterial contamination unless the company for which they work has a training session that includes this information. Happily, most eating establishments have good records of food processing and storage, and employees who are at least somewhat aware of proper personal hygiene and sanitation.

A compilation of common-sense precautions can be found at many food-preparation sites (Table 8.2). The table's last statement should be our guidepost: when in doubt, throw it out.

9

Concerns for the Future: Botulism and Bioterrorism

It is sometimes difficult to tell if an event is a cause for concern or represents a hope for the future. Such is the case with the numbers provided by the Centers for Disease Control and Prevention (CDC) regarding the number of cases of botulism reported over the last few years. Since 2000, the total number of cases has ranged from a high of 170 cases in 2006 to a low of 107 in 2004. While 2004 represents the lowest figures in a decade, the numbers shown in Table 9.1 suggest that this may not represent a downward trend. Closer inspection of the CDC data for 2001 shows that 15 of the cases involved contaminated chili from Texas, and 20 cases were from the Pacific Northwest.

BIOTERROR CONCERNS: HISTORICAL PRECEDENTS

Bioterrorism is often defined as any actual or threatened use of micro-organisms or their products (toxins) designed to cause death or disease in animals, humans, or plants. Attempts to use the botulinum toxin as a weapon of war have been documented since the 1930s. The Japanese fed their Manchurian prisoners cultures of *Clostridium botulinum*. During World War II, the Japanese biological warfare group, known as Unit 731, did the same to their Chinese prisoners, each time killing the prisoners. On three known occasions between 1990 and 1995, the Japanese cult *Aum Shinrikyo* made attempts to spread botulinum toxin through the air. They

Table 9.1 Cases of Botulism in the United States, 2000–2007

	Foodborne	Infant	Other	TOTAL
2000	23	93	22	138
2001	39	97	20	156
2002	26	66	19	111
2003	19	71	30	120
2004	19	75	13	107
2005	18	96	28	142
2006	19	106	45	170
2007	32	87	25	144

Source: Data compiled from *Morbidity and Mortality Weekly Reports*, Centers for Disease Control and Prevention.

obtained their *C. botulinum* from soil they collected in northern Japan.

During World War II, the Allies became concerned that Germany had made a weapon of botulinum toxin. Consequently, Allied troops were vaccinated with the toxoid vaccine available at the time. More than one million doses of botulinum toxoid vaccine were prepared for the troops that would invade France on June 6, 1944. The United States had produced, but never used, botulinum toxin as a potential weapon during World War II. This weapons program was ended after the Biological and Toxin Weapons Convention in 1972.

The report produced by the Biological and Toxin Weapons Convention prohibited offensive research and development of biological weapons. More than 100 nations including Iraq and the Soviet Union signed the document. However, the evidence is clear that the former Soviet Union carried out research and collaborated with Iraq on the weaponization of botulinum toxin into the early 1990s.

One outcome of the 1991 Persian Gulf War was the admission by Iraq to the United Nations inspection team that the regime had produced 19,000 liters (5,019.27 gallons) of concentrated botulinum toxin. More chilling was the admission that approximately 10,000 liters (2,641.72 gallons) had been loaded into various military weapons. If one-third of those 19,000 liters were inhaled, it would kill everyone in the world. A single gram (0.04 oz.) could kill one million people. The toxin prevents nerve endings from sending signals to the muscles, which leads to paralysis. Paralyzing muscles of the respiratory system leads to the need for a ventilator for the patient for periods of more than six weeks. The impact of a bioterror attack using the toxin would have a devastating impact on medical services.

CATEGORIZATION OF BIOTERROR AGENTS

The CDC have designated three categories for bioterror agents. Botulism is classified in Category A, which is the highest priority category for a potential bioterror agent. In short, these are the organisms that are most dangerous as possible bioterror agents. Botulism meets the criteria set up by the CDC:

- The agent is easily disseminated or transmitted from person to person.

- It results in high mortality rate and has the potential for major public health impact.

- It might cause panic or social disruption.

- It requires special action for public health preparedness.

Included in Category A are the agents of smallpox, anthrax, plague, botulism, tularemia, and viral hemorrhagic fevers.

Category B diseases/agents are the second highest priority agents and include those that are moderately easy to disseminate, result in moderate morbidity rates and low mortality rates, and require specific enhancements of CDC's diagnostic capacity and enhanced disease surveillance. In this group are the salmonellas, the cholera organism, and a number of other disease organisms that cause everything from food poisoning to severe diarrhea.

Category C diseases/agents are the third highest priority agents and include emerging pathogens that could be engineered for mass dissemination in the future because of availability, ease of production and dissemination, and potential for high morbidity and mortality rates and major health impact. A number of viruses such as the hantavirus are in this group.

NIAID RESEARCH AT THE GENETIC LEVEL

The National Institute of Allergy and Infectious Diseases (NIAID) is part of the U.S. Department of Health and Human Services. Because bioterrorism continues to be a real concern for the United States, NIAID and other agencies have accelerated microbial research and development of diagnostic, preventive, and treatment methods. Microbial **genomics** has become an important part of this overall approach. Genomics refers to being able to identify and utilize the totality of genetic information found in an organism. This complete collection of an organism's genetic information is known as its **genome**. Understanding an organism's genetic program may aid in understanding how an organism carries out its biochemical and physical processing and operates as a complex biological system.

According to the National Institutes of Health (NIH), this genetic information is used to develop gene-based diagnostic and sampling tests to quickly detect dangerous germs and assess their susceptibility to different types of treatment. Genomes also provide molecular fingerprints of different strains of a given microbe, thereby enabling investigators to better track future outbreaks to their source.

In May 2004, the Sanger Institute completed the sequence of the genome of *Clostridium botulinum* in collaboration with Dr. Roger Huston of the University of Reading, Dr. Nigel Minton of the University of Nottingham, and Dr. M. Peck of the Institute of Food Research.

NIAID RESEARCH AGAINST BACTERIAL PRODUCTS

NIAID is involved in both long- and short-term biodefense research studies to find ways to deal with infectious microbial diseases caused by microbial toxins. Toxins that have potential use as bioterror agents are particularly highlighted. A major part of the research is to develop FDA-approved vaccines, treatments, and diagnostic tests that could be used as part of a defensive package against these bioterror agents. The research goals of NIAID for botulism include developing an enhanced package of antitoxins for the treatment of botulism, a vaccine that will be effective against all seven types of botulinum toxins, and better methods of detecting and diagnosing the illness. NIAID is also working with the U.S. Department of Defense, CDC, and U.S. Department of Energy to develop rapid diagnosis/detection PCR (polymerase chain reaction) assays, a type of test that can detect the bacteria's toxin DNA sequences (current tests can detect the presence of the *C. botulinum* gene, but cannot tell if it is releasing toxins), and test standard poison detoxification techniques to determine the ones that can best reduce or eliminate the number of toxins circulating in the blood.

SOME CAUTIONARY TALES

The Laboratory Response Network

The Laboratory Response Network (LRN) is a national network of more than 120 laboratories that receives samples from local health departments and local practitioners. It has been developed to coordinate all clinical diagnostic testing for suspected bioterrorism events. When a patient is suspected to have botulism, his or her samples of stool, serum, or other materials are sent for testing to a lab that is part of the LRN, which is organized into three laboratory levels (sentinel, reference, and national). There were originally four categories, labeled A, B, C, and D (Figure 9.1). Each response level has access to standardized protocols to test for agents of bioterrorism, including *C. botulinum* and botulinum toxins.

The LRN relies on voluntary cooperation among laboratories. It requires that labs assess their capabilities relative to the biosafety requirements (Table 9.2) needed to perform the types of analysis normally done by labs at biosafety levels A and B. LRN national laboratories (formerly level D) have BSL-4 containment facilities. Currently, the only laboratories so designated are at the CDC and the U.S. Army Medical Research Institute of Infectious Diseases (USAMRIID) located at Fort Dedrick, Maryland. National laboratories function to "confirm, validate, and archive" bioterrorism agents.

Laboratory Biosafety

Botulinum toxin and *Clostridium* species that produce botulinum toxin are classified as select agents and regulated under 42 CFR part 73 (Possession, Use, and Transfer of Select Agents and Toxins), which was published as an Interim Final Rule in the *Federal Register* on December 13, 2002. As specified in the Public Health Security and Bioterrorism Preparedness and Response Act of 2002, 42 CFR part 73 provides requirements for laboratories that handle select agents (including registration, security risk assessments, safety plans, security plans, emergency response plans, training, transfers, record keeping, inspections, and notifications). These new requirements went into effect on February 7, 2003, and override earlier government requirements regarding possession and transfer of select agents. The FDA has published biosafety recommendations for laboratories that test for *C. botulinum*.

The Public Health Security and Bioterrorism Preparedness and Response Act also led to a reorganization of the LRN. There are now three levels of laboratories that are part of the network. Each level utilizes standard procedures for testing bioterrorism agents, including botulinum toxins. The CDC/NIH have developed a series of protocols for these laboratories entitled *Biosafety in Microbiological and Biomedical Laboratories.*

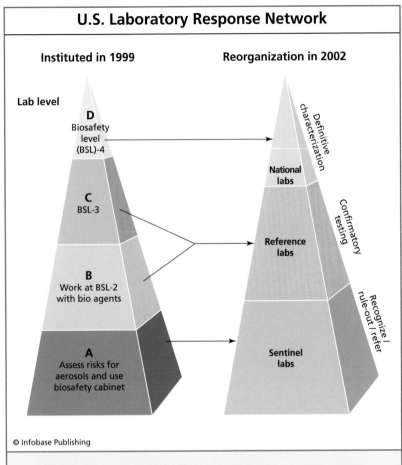

Figure 9.1 The Laboratory Response Network is an integrated network of state and local public health, federal, military, and international laboratories. These labs can respond to bioterrorism, chemical terrorism, and other public health emergencies.

Labs formerly known as Level A are now LRN sentinel laboratories. Most clinical laboratories with at least BSL-2 containment fall into this category and function as laboratory first-responders that rule out those diseases which do not qualify for inclusion. Sentinel laboratories would collect appropriate specimens for the detection of *C. botulinum* and/or its toxin

Table 9.2 Summary of Recommended Biosafety Levels (BSL) for Infectious Agents

BSL	Agents	Practices	Safety Equipment (Primary Barriers)	Facilities (Secondary Barriers)
1	Not known to cause disease in healthy adults	Standard Microbiological Practices	None required	Open bench-top sink required
2	Associated with human disease; autoinoculation, ingestion, mucous membrane exposure	BSL-1 practice plus: • Limited access • Biohazard warning signs • Sharps precautions • Biosafety manual defining any needed waste, decontamination or medical surveillance policies	Primary barriers; Class I or II Biosafety Cabinets (BSCs) or other physical containment devices used for all manipulations of agents that cause splashes or aerosols of infectious materials; Personal Protective Equipment (PPEs): laboratory coats, gloves, face protection as needed	BSL-1 plus: Autoclave available
3	Indigenous or exotic agents with potential for aerosol transmission; disease may have serious or lethal consequences	BSL-2 practice plus: • Controlled access • Decontamination of lab clothing before laundering • Baseline serum	Primary barriers; Class I or II BSCs or other physical containment devices used for all manipulations of agents; PPEs: protective lab clothing, gloves, respiratory protection is needed	BSL-2 plus: • Physical separation from access corridors • Self-closing, double door access • Exhausted air not recirculated—Negative airflow into laboratory
4	Dangerous/exotic agents that pose high risk of life-threatening disease; aerosol-transmitted lab infections; related agents with unknown risk of transmission	BSL-3 practices plus: • Clothing change before entering • Shower on exit • All material decontaminated on exit from facility	Primary barriers; all procedures conducted in Class III BSCs or Class I or II BSCs in combination with full-body, air-supplied, positive pressure personnel suit	BSL-3 plus: • Separate building or isolated zone • Dedicated supply/exhaust, vacuum, and decontamination systems • Other requirements outlined in the text

Source: Data compiled from *Morbidity and Mortality Weekly Reports*, Centers for Disease Control and Prevention.

FDA BIOSAFETY RECOMMENDATIONS FOR LABS THAT TEST FOR *C. BOTULINUM*

- Place biohazard signs on doors to restrict entrance and keep the number of people in the laboratory to a minimum.

- All workers should wear laboratory coats and safety glasses.

- Never pipette anything by mouth; use mechanical pipettes.

- Use a biohazard hood for transfer of toxic material, if possible.

- Centrifuge toxic materials in a hermetically closed centrifuge with safety cups.

- Personally take all toxic material to the autoclave and see that it is sterilized immediately.

- Do not work alone in the laboratory or animal rooms after hours or on weekends.

- Have an eyewash fountain and foot-pedaled faucet available for hand washing.

- Allow no eating or drinking in the laboratory.

- In a very visible location, list phone numbers where therapeutic antitoxin can be obtained. Reduce clutter in the laboratory to a minimum and keep all equipment and other materials in their proper place.

and consult the state public health laboratory to determine where specimens should be sent (i.e., the nearest LRN reference laboratory with appropriate expertise).

LRN reference laboratories (formerly Levels B and C) are mostly state or local public health laboratories with BSL-3 containment facilities. They have the expertise and equipment that allows them access to nonpublic testing protocols and reagents. These laboratories function to "rule-in and refer." Reference laboratories conduct botulinum toxin detection and typing plus *C. botulinum* culture and identification. The confirmation of a clinical diagnosis of botulism needs to be done as rapidly as possible, so specimens should be sent directly to the nearest reference laboratory with capacity for botulinum toxin testing, as identified by the state public health laboratory.

The third category is the LRN national laboratories (formerly Level D) with BSL-4 containment facilities. National laboratories are the final link in the confirmation of a disease organism being used as a bioterrorism agent.

Given the importance of these laboratories and the stringent nature of the laboratory protocols involved, it was upsetting when three laboratory technicians working at a BSL-2 level laboratory in Boston, Massachusetts, became infected with a lethal strain of an organism that causes the disease known as tularemia. The technicians were trying to develop a vaccine and thought they had been working with a harmless strain. Unfortunately, a lethal strain had been mixed in with the harmless one. Tularemia is classified as a Category A agent in the same category as botulism.

The illnesses were made public in January 2005, but had occurred in May and September of 2004. Boston currently has 800 BSL-2 labs, about 12 BSL-3 labs, and opened an additional BSL-4 lab at Boston University in 2009. These laboratory accidents and the subsequent delay in notification to the public have raised concern and a number of safety-related questions about the new laboratory. This is not the only accident in BSL laboratories and a number of incidents have been discovered at the BSL-4 laboratory at Fort Dedrick, Maryland.

THE SPREAD OF BOTOX

While certainly not of the same magnitude of concern as a bioterror weapon, the increasing number of uses of botulinum toxin has become a cause of concern within the medical community. In an attempt to find ever more uses for Botox, it has been injected into numerous muscular and glandular sites throughout the body. Someone suggested that Botox was medicine's answer to duct tape.[1] Dr. Mitchell F. Brin, chief scientific officer for Botox's maker Allergan, has suggested that no other therapeutic agent "has so many demonstrated uses."

However, consumer advocacy groups are concerned that these new uses are occurring before clinical trials have determined proper dosages for the new treatments. The health research group at consumer advocacy group Public Citizen has petitioned the FDA to require a warning label for injectable toxins. Dr. Kamran Jafri, a facial surgeon in Manhattan, uses Botox injections to reduce pore size and oily skin. "Dosing is by trial and error. I don't think it's experimental because I've been doing it a lot and it's been working," says Dr. Jamfri. Most scientists would not see this as comforting or as providing proof of safety.[2]

On April 30, 2009, the FDA announced it would require a warning, known as black box labeling, on Botox and similar products because of concerns about a rare but potentially deadly complication that can occur when the toxin spreads beyond the injection site. In addition to the warning label, the manufacturers will also be required to:

- Inform users in writing about the potential risk for distant spread at the time of injection.

- Warn doctors and patients about the risks associated with substituting one botulism product for another. The products have different dosing units, which are incompatible, so switching products can result in dangerous overdosing. Follow a group of children and adults using Botox or similar products off-label to

treat involuntary muscle movement and submit safety
data to the agency.

The FDA has indicated little concern about safety when
the drugs are used as directed for cosmetic purposes. When
drugs are used for purposes other than those approved and in
ways that have not been subjected to rigorous clinical testing,
patients are placed at unacceptable risk.[3]

UNEXPECTED CHEMICALS IN OUR ENVIRONMENT

The concerns noted by researchers at Stanford University (see
"Be Careful of What You Smell" on page 104)—that chemicals
in the environment may have negative effects on humans—are
echoed in a report by Bill Battaglin and Lori Sprague who
work for the U.S. Geological Survey. They analyzed 125 water
samples taken between October 2002 and September 2003
in Colorado. They found a number of chemicals, such as fire
retardants, steroids, prescription drugs, insecticides, pesticides,
and caffeine, were found in water sources, ranging from drinking water wells to streams, groundwater, and even remote areas
in the Colorado mountains. While regulated chemicals had
acceptable safety limits, there were no standards for most of the
62 chemicals that were discovered in the water.

A number of these unregulated chemicals are known to
cause increased resistance to antibiotics and interfere with
proper reproduction in fish. The study was designed as a starting point to determine the direct and indirect impact of these
chemicals on humans.

The presence of these chemicals in the waters of Colorado
is of particular concern because the state has one of the highest incidences of botulism in the nation due to the pH of soil
and its high altitude. In addition, many of these chemicals are
known to disrupt proper functioning of the immune system and
in combination with an illness like botulism would reduce the
chance of recovery from the disease. Many of these chemicals

BE CAREFUL OF WHAT YOU SMELL: DOES IT SMELL TOO GOOD TO BE GOOD?

One great concern among many scientists is the number of synthetic chemicals that are being added to the environment. The science of ecotoxicology attempts to determine how these chemicals affect the earth's systems. Researchers at Stanford University made some disquieting discoveries about the unintended impact of certain chemicals, while testing the effects of synthetic musk compounds on defense systems of mussels.

The researchers exposed live mussels to low concentrations of six commercial musks that are used to improve the smell of everything from detergents and soap to air fresheners and shampoo. These, as well as other synthetic fragrances, are routinely being added to our environment. As expected, the musk chemicals did not poison the mussels. The mussels were then placed in clean water, which removed all of the musk chemicals. The mussels were transferred to clean water that had a red dye added to it. Cells of the mussels have a mechanism to detect a foreign substance, such as the dye, and keep it out. The unexpected outcome was that the mussels took up the red dye. It appears that they had lost their natural defense. Mussels that had not been exposed to the musk chemicals retained the ability to repel the dye molecules. "This is the first line of defense used by all cells," said David Epel, one of the Stanford researchers. "It consists of a special protein, called an efflux transporter, that's embedded in the cell membrane and pumps out toxins that get into the cell."

The California Sea Grant program provided a portion of the funding for the study. Their report indicated alarm since the cells of many animal groups, including humans, use the same or similar protective mechanisms to fight off foreign substances. While these chemicals are not directly toxic to an organism, they appear to increase its sensitivity to toxic agents in the environment. The finding raises concerns that these very common household compounds may pose unanticipated environmental and human health risks. Cell functioning continued to be impaired 24 to 48 hours after exposure ended, which the scientists called "troubling" since it implies that brief events, such as sewage or chemical spills, could have lasting environmental effects.

The buildup of these chemicals represents a potential public health risk. "People have these same transporters in the blood-brain barrier, the placenta, and the intestines," explained Till Luckenbach, another of the Stanford researchers. "Perhaps exposure to chemical fragrances could compromise the transporters, making it easier for pollutants to enter the brain, for example." They build up in human tissue, as well as the tissues of human food sources such as fish and invertebrates like mussels.

What is the probability that additional damage to our protective systems from such chemicals will make it possible for new weapons of bioterror to arise from those which we are currently protected from? "One of the assumptions about these chemicals is that they are regarded as environmentally low risk compared to pesticides and oil products," Epel said. "This is the first study to show that some personal care products in water do have an effect, even in low concentrations. Our results indicate that the effects on the first line of defense might be irreversible or continue long after the event. It's a warning sign. It's a smoking gun. Are there other chemicals out there that have similar long-term effects? Could these be harming these defense systems in aquatic organisms? And could they be having similar effects in humans?"

may allow other normal bacteria to mutate and work with the botulism organism to produce a synergistic disease effect where the impact of the two organisms together would be greater than the combined impact of each separately.

There is a particularly high count of Type A *C. botulinum* spores in the soil of the regions from the Rocky Mountains to the Pacific Ocean. This type of spore produces the most dangerous human toxin. A second, and probably more important, reason for the increased botulism cases in Colorado has to do with the relationship between temperature and altitude. Colorado is a high-altitude state, and the temperature of boiling water decreases as the altitude increases. Central Colorado is more than a mile high and most ski resorts are more than two miles high. In other words, water will boil at a lower temperature in Colorado than it will in a low-altitude state such as Georgia. Thus, the temperature at which foods are processed is lower. To make sure that a proper canning temperature is reached, the pressure must be adjusted. The canning pressure for low-acid foods must be increased by 0.5 pounds (226.8 g) for every 1,000 feet (304.8 m) rise in elevation. For example, at 5,000 feet (1,524 m) vegetables must be pressure canned at 12.5 pounds (5.67 kg) pressure per square inch (6.45 sq. cm) rather than the usual 10 pounds (4.54 kg) recommended in canning instructions designed for sea-level canning. If a person does not make these changes, their food will not be properly processed and they would be at an increased risk of botulism.

It seems unfortunate that we spend so much money on materials and methods to protect us from bioterrorism and yet we continue to be ignorant about basic food safety procedures in our homes and workplaces. It also seems clear that environmental factors can increase the severity or transmission of disease organisms and yet we continue to ignore this entire area of study. Unless we are willing to identify and deal with long-term environmental changes that can exacerbate the spread of infectious diseases, we will be unable to deal completely with the challenges presented by these disease organisms.

10

Hopes for the Future

MOLECULAR DETECTION OF
CLOSTRIDIUM BOTULINUM AND ITS TOXINS

In the mid-1960s, television viewers were introduced to a new science fiction series called *Star Trek*. One of the main characters was Dr. Leonard McCoy, the ship's doctor, played by the late DeForest Kelley. One of his medical instruments was a handheld device called a tricorder. He would pass the tricorder over the body of the patient to detect, identify, and analyze a number of bodily functions and various chemicals. In March 2000, at the annual meeting of the American Chemical Society, the Department of Energy's Sandia National Laboratories in Livermore, California, unveiled its own prototype of the tricorder. Officially called an integrated MicroChemLab, the device can analyze a complex mixture of chemicals in approximately one minute. A small screen indicates the name and quantity of the chemicals at a level of parts per billion.

In December 2004, Sandia National Laboratories introduced its latest rendition of the MicroChemLab. A red, three-pound device that can detect viruses, bacteria, or biological toxins within seconds to minutes, it is designed to provide a rapid method of testing the purity of a water supply. The device uses a technique pioneered for the detection of DNA, commonly called DNA fingerprinting. In this case, proteins are being "fingerprinted." Different toxins, bacteria, and viruses have differing amounts of unique proteins that this fingerprinting method can identify (Figure 10.1).

In a related press release issued in October 2003, Affymetrix, Inc., announced that it was developing a test that could detect many of the major bacterial and viral agents that constitute biological threats. The Biodefense Microarray Test is a single-step test capable of detecting, in four

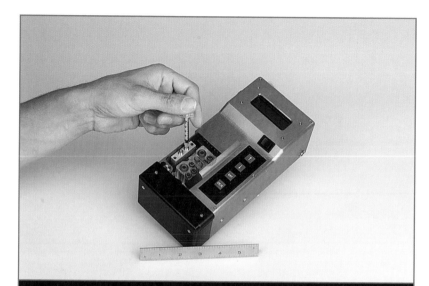

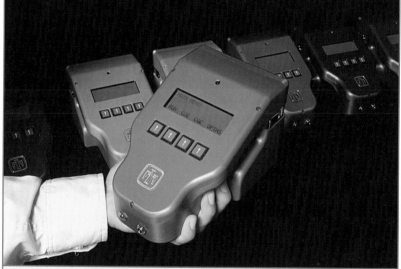

Figure 10.1 MicroChemLab, seen here, is the equivalent of full-scale biochemistry laboratory. One variant of the device can detect and identify biotoxins, viruses, and bacterial agents. A second variant can detect chemical warfare agents and select toxic industrial chemicals, explosives, and organic solvents. (Courtesy of Sandia National Laboratories)

hours or less, the genetic fingerprints of 26 different bacterial and 10 viral species, as well as hundreds of subspecies. The microarray will be able to detect up to 56 different bacterial genes that lead to production of toxins.

This method could potentially enable us to detect a deadly gene inserted into a harmless bacterium. In addition to its use in biodefense, similar microarrays will find their way into doctors' offices, providing rapid diagnosis of patient illnesses. Microarrays are already available for *C. botulinum* that allow for detection of the organisms within food particles.

In 2003, researchers at the University of Ulster in Northern Ireland announced they had developed a DNA fingerprinting technique that would speed up detection of microbes that might be put into food or water. The test looks for a specific gene or DNA segment that would be present in naturally occurring pathogens in food or water. The scientists involved suggest that they can determine the type and source of the agent within 15 minutes, thus providing an early warning detection system.

AS THE WORM TURNS

At the University of Georgia (UGA), microscopic worms called nematodes are being used as test organisms to determine chemical toxicity. Dr. Phil Williams is an environmental health scientist working with these worms in hopes of reducing the number of mice and other large organisms needed for chemical testing. The nematode he is using is from the genus *Caenorhabditis,* and is already famous as the test organism that resulted in the 2002 Nobel Prize in Physiology and Medicine for Dr. John Sulston, Dr. Sydney Brenner, and Dr. H. Robert Horvitz. While the worms are not expected to replace higher animals completely, they are proving effective in the early stages of toxicity testing. They provide an inexpensive and rapid method for screening chemicals that are being considered for use throughout the chemical industry.

Because the worm is a normal soil organism, Williams uses it to predict environmental effects of chemical exposure or when testing soil for toxic results. Williams is also working with other UGA scientists to adapt nematodes for use in detection of foodborne pathogens such as *Clostridium botulinum*. It is hoped that these worms will provide useful animal models for predicting chemical effects on humans and their environment.

NEW LABS

In September 2003, the UGA Department of Food Science and Technology opened its new building addition and renovated spaces including state-of-the-art microbiology laboratories. The biocontainment Level-3 lab makes it possible for UGA scientists to work with biohazards such as botulism. UGA has become a major player in cutting-edge research on food safety and food processing. The building was the second of three initiatives funded by the Food Processing Advisory Council (FOODPAC) that are part of the university's system of infrastructure improvements. Agriculture is the largest industry in Georgia, representing more than $5.7 billion dollars annually, and industry leaders wanted to be sure that their investments would be safeguarded for the future. The first initiative was the expansion of the UGA Center for Food Safety in Griffin, Georgia. The third and final project was the construction of Georgia Tech's Food Processing Technology Building, completed in 2005.

NEW DIAGNOSTIC TESTS

IGEN International, Inc., announced that the United States Department of Agriculture's (USDA) Food Safety and Inspection Service (FSIS) was purchasing its botulinum toxin test. While most of the details of the test are confidential, it is based on the process of electrochemiluminescence. This is a process where certain chemical compounds emit light when electrochemically stimulated. The technology that uses this process is called Origen technology and was patented by IGEN. The FSIS is the public health arm of the USDA. The job of the FSIS is to check commercial supplies of meat, poultry, and egg products to determine if they have been properly labeled and packaged and if they are safe according to all applicable federal regulations. This purchase is part of the USDA's Homeland Security Program on food safety. These diagnostic tests will eventually be available to commercial customers outside the government.

Dr. Weihong Tan and his research team at the University of Florida used specially treated nanoparticles of silica to detect a single *Escherichia coli* bacterium in a sample of ground beef. A nanoparticle is one billionth of a meter. Silica is the common name for the chemical silicon dioxide. It is hard and insoluble, and appears in nature as crystals of quartz. The research team attached antibodies specific to the *E. coli* strain to silica particles that measured 60 nanometers in diameter. Attached to these particles were thousands of fluorescent dye molecules. When the meat sample was mixed with the fluorescent silica nanoparticles, the antibodies attached to the *E. coli* and the dye molecules could be detected. The scientists hope that by changing the antibodies used, they will be able to detect a variety of bacterial pathogens, including *C. botulinum.*

Dr. Richard Durst, professor of chemistry at Cornell University, developed a test strip that can be placed in a sample solution to determine if botulinum toxin is present. The sample solution contains molecules of a lipid or fatty materials which is the natural receptor for the botulinum toxin in the cell membrane. A red dye is attached to the fat molecules. Antibotulinum antibodies that will neutratlize the toxin on contact are attached to a special cellulose strip. The sample to be tested is mixed with the solution containing the fat molecules and dye. The strip is inserted into the solution. If the toxin is present, it will attach to the dyed fat molecules and also be attached to the antibodies on the strip. The presence of the toxin causes a visible red line within 15 to 20 minutes. New information about ribonucleic acid (**RNA**) molecules is also being considered as a means of detecting or eliminating various protein toxins.

RIBOSWITCHES

The importance of RNA as a messenger of coded information, which tells how to construct a specific protein, has been known since 1953. Cells use part of **deoxyribonucleic acid's (DNA)** genetic information to produce molecules of RNA. One type, known as **messenger RNA (mRNA)**, carries the genetic information to the surface of the cell's workbenches called ribosomes. Based on this coded information, specific **amino acids** are properly positioned and bonded together to form the basic structure of a protein.

Eventually, additional jobs were associated with RNA. It was shown that RNA could regulate the rate of biochemical reactions and not be used up in the reaction. This job in cells was originally thought to be the exclusive domain of proteins called enzymes. These RNA molecules with enzyme-like qualities are called **ribozymes**. Ronald Breaker of Yale University has worked with synthetic ribozymes for a number of years. Breaker has created strands of mRNA that can find and attach to specific small molecules. These RNAs, called **aptamers,** function like protein antibodies and might prove useful in diagnostic tests similar to ones that use antibodies.

Breaker's research team began to search for naturally occurring aptamers. Based on the success of the artificial aptamers, it seemed likely that naturally occurring RNAs might be found that regulate gene action by attaching to the product of the gene's information. In this way, the RNA would act as a control switch. Breaker's team dubbed these RNA molecules **riboswitches**. Riboswitches are sections of mRNA molecules that do not contain code for protein production. These noncoding regions are also known as untranslated regions. They can function as highly specific receptors for small molecules. Riboswitches occur naturally in the noncoding regions of many bacterial messenger RNAs where they function as genetic switches. When the RNA riboswitch attaches to a specific target molecule, the entire mRNA strand changes shape. In this way, production of proteins is either started or stopped.

So far, researchers have found riboswitches that respond to changes in temperature or concentrations of small molecules such as vitamins or amino acids. This allows organisms to sense, and then respond to, changes in their environment by regulating their gene activity. Recently, a riboswitch affecting the synthesis of the amino acid methionine has been discovered in the pathogenic clostridia, including *C. botulinum*.

At least eight families of riboswitches have been found in bacteria. In 2003, Japanese researchers identified a riboswitch in a fungus, a eukaryote that has cells organized in the same way as plants, animals, and people. This suggests a whole new area of research involving genetic control mechanisms in higher organisms.

Biologists hope they will be able to use riboswitches in diagnostic tests that detect small amounts of bacterial proteins. Antibiotics that act like bacterial riboswitches could cause the bacteria to turn off production of an essential protein and, thus, starve themselves to death.

PROJECT BIOSHIELD

Project BioShield legislation was signed into law by President George W. Bush in July 2004. It enables the federal government to spend up to $5.6 billion over a 10-year period to purchase drugs and vaccines from biotechnology and pharmaceutical companies. Botulinum toxin is included in the list of pathogenic and infectious agents that are covered by the shield. The project allows the National Institutes of Health (NIH) to circumvent traditional procedures for granting research and development grants and contracts to industries. The project also allows the FDA to distribute experimental drugs in case of emergencies, such as bioterrorist attacks, without the usual approval methods.

So far, none of the government money has been released for spending. Most biotechnology and pharmaceutical companies are waiting for additional legislation that would protect them from being sued in case a drug or vaccine they make has an adverse health effect. Project BioShield merely spends money for drugs and vaccines; it does not fund any basic research or soften the risk to companies that decide to develop a product, which the government is under no obligation to buy. Most companies don't like the risk involved.

Fortunately, the National Institute of Allergy and Infectious Diseases (NIAID), a division of the NIH, still has money to spend on funding of various research projects. In July 2004, NIAID provided two research project grants that will be awarded in 6 months rather than the usual 12 to 18 months. The speedup is part of the BioShield regulations. The grants will still be peer-reviewed and will be available to scientists in both industry and academia. The first grant will provide $10 million toward development of potential vaccines, diagnostic tests, and other therapeutic materials for Category A pathogens, including *C. botulinum*.

PROTECTION BEFORE AND AFTER DETECTION

Active research into the development of drugs and vaccines that will destroy or inactivate botulinum toxins is ongoing. At Brookhaven National Laboratories in Upton, New York, researchers have developed a chemical inhibitor of the botulinum toxin. The inhibitor causes the toxin's structure to become modified, so that it can no longer attach to its target molecules. A zinc ion present within the binding site of the toxin is moved to a different section of the toxin molecule, causing the toxin to lose its functional ability. It is hoped that this drug may be useful as a means of protection, either as a vaccine or as a therapeutic aid after exposure.

THE PARADOX OF TOXINS

In many ways, botulinum toxins represent a paradox. They are one of the six Class A agents that represent a tremendous public health threat if they were to be weaponized. Yet these same toxins at lower concentrations are used for a number of medical and cosmetic treatments. Botox is well known to the public. There is a relatively easy accessibility to the toxins for legitimate purposes, which also means easy access for less than legitimate reasons. In addition, people who have repeated injections of Botox may become hypersensitive to the protein that is the toxin. If these people needed to be vaccinated against the toxins, it might prove deadly since the vaccines contain the botulinum proteins. Thus, mass vaccinations against botulism would prevent people from receiving the Botox injections or any other therapies that might involve the use of the botulinum proteins.

While most of our understanding of the uses of Botox involves cosmetic repair, a new therapeutic use has been described. It has been known that Botox injections can help certain victims of muscular diseases regain control of spasmodic muscles. We are now seeing off-label use of Botox for stroke victims. Off label means that this use is not currently approved by the FDA. Despite this lack of approval by the FDA, Medicare and most health care insurers are reimbursing users for the cost of the procedure. Unfortunately, few doctors are currently trained to do these procedures, which involve deeper injections than those involved in removing wrinkles. Botox cannot bring back use to muscles whose controlling brain region has been destroyed. But stroke victims receiving these injections look and feel better and have greater control of their muscles, allowing them to feed, bathe, and clothe themselves.[1]

ANIMAL VACCINES

Botulism also affects animals other than humans. Vaccines exist and are in current use for cattle, minks, and horses. In 2000, a group of Florida researchers started the Regal Swan project (Figure 10.2). Their purpose was to prevent worldwide mortality of swans due to botulism. In 2002, the six Florida researchers confirmed that the vaccine used against botulism in swans has been highly successful in showing a sustained level of antibody

Figure 10.2 English mute swans. Researchers with the Regal Swan Project developed and tested a highly successful vaccine that provides hope that the world's largest waterfowl can be protected from botulism. (© Maksym Gorpenyuk/shutterstock images)

response. The group's research offers the first real hope that a vaccine against the deadly *Clostridia* bacterial toxin can protect the world's largest waterfowl. According to the group, the three-year scientific study and more than 20 years of clinical trial of vaccine usage in swans produced no detrimental side effects or deaths in inoculated swans.

HUMAN VACCINES AND THE FUTURE

As of early 2010, there were no botulism vaccines available for the public. An experimental vaccine has been available since 1979 for laboratory workers and military personnel. This particular vaccine requires multiple injections over the course of a year, making it an unlikely candidate for use on a large scale.

According to Leonard A. Smith, chief of the Department of Immunology and Molecular Biology, Division of Toxicology and Aerobiology, United States Army Medical Research Institute of Infectious Diseases (USAMRIID), there are additional problems with this vaccine. High costs are associated with the vaccine's production since it requires a facility that meets stringent manufacturing and safety requirements that include the prevention of viral or bacterial contamination during any part of the manufacturing process. Additionally, the current vaccine does not protect against all of the seven botulism proteins, and the level of protection varies for each of the proteins that are used. The current pentavalent vaccine acts against toxins A, B, C, D, and E. It is most effective against toxins A and B.

Attempts to develop a botulism vaccine had been ongoing. In 1996, the U.S. Army awarded a three-year renewable contract to Mike Meagher, a biochemical engineer at the University of Nebraska's Lincoln campus. He holds joint appointments in the departments of food science and technology and biological systems engineering at the university. His original contract involved developing processes to produce anti-botulism vaccines for the USAMRIID. Prior to the 1990 Desert Storm operation, the army developed a botulism vaccine that was to be used to treat soldiers, if necessary. The army injected 100 horses with botulinum toxin so that the horses would produce antibodies against the botulinum proteins. The resulting serum would contain the antibodies necessary to destroy the botulinum protein toxins, but would also contain horse proteins that the human immune system might react to in a negative way. Thus, there was a concern about the compatibility of the horse vaccine with humans. In addition, victims using the horse serum would need to be treated within two hours of exposure for the vaccine to be effective.

Meagher's research group was to be responsible for developing the vaccine's entire production process. This early work has led to the University of Nebraska at Lincoln being one of the research teams that is currently working with USAMRIID and DynPort

Vaccine Company to develop two botulism vaccines. DynPort is the major contractor, and the University of Nebraska is one of four research specialist groups involved with the project.

In September 2003, Dr. James Nataro and his colleagues at the University of Maryland's Center for Vaccine Development were awarded a 4 1/2-year agreement to develop a number of single dose vaccines. The group of vaccines included those against anthrax, plague, and botulism.

In October 2004, DynPort entered clinical trials with its new botulinum vaccine. The trials involve healthy individuals between 18 to 40 years of age.

On January 14, 2005, Emergent BioSolutions and Health Protection Agency (HPA) of Great Britain announced a two-year licensing and development agreement to produce a botulism vaccine. Both of these companies have histories of developing novel vaccines for preventive and therapeutic use against biological weapons.

In 2006, the Cangene Corporation of Winnipeg, Canada, was awarded a five-year contract by the Department of Health and Human Services to provide 200,000 doses of a botulism antitoxin. The contract amounted to over $360 million and the company has delivered the antitoxin to the Strategic National Stockpile. The Department of Homeland Security determined the amount of the antitoxin to be purchased based on their analysis of the country's need for biodefense preparedness against botulinum toxin.

In April 2009, Cambridge Biostability and DynPort Vaccine Company announced the successful production of a thermally stable, rapidly injectable, pentavalent recombinant botulinum vaccine candidate. Their vaccine candidate is designed to provide protection against exposure to botulinum neurotoxin serotypes A, B, C, E, and F.

A number of new and narrowly focused vaccines are being developed to fight the various toxins that make up the disease known as botulism. These attempts are using new methods and materials that will reduce the potential side effects of most vaccines, mainly delayed hypersenitivity reactions that can lead to anaphylactic shock and death. Progress is also being made in creating vaccines for other animal species. While most of the initiatives toward vaccines and increased food safety have been stimulated by the fear of bioterrorism, the end results will be useful to all people in all parts of the world. We continue to see progress in the areas of molecular biology and the various types of microarrays that are becoming more available and less expensive. Perhaps it will soon be possible to have a new meaning when we say we have put our stamp of approval on something. With these new arrays, we can detect minute levels of contaminants in less than an hour by merely sticking the sensor into the food.

In spite of all of our technology, our best weapon in the fight against disease organisms and their products will continue to be an informed public with five active senses and more than a smidgin of common sense and good personal hygiene.

Notes

Chapter 2

1. Food and Drug Administration, "Guidance for Industry: Refrigerated Carrot Juice and Other Refrigerated Low-Acid Juices, http://www.fda.gov/Food/GuidanceComplianceRegulatoryInformation/GuidanceDocuments/Juice/ucm072481.htm, accessed October 15, 2009; Shuler et al., "Botulism Associated with Commercial Carrot Juice—Georgia and Florida, 2006," *Morbidity and Mortality Weekly Report* 55 (October 6, 2006): 1–2.

2. Castleberry's, "Expanded Voluntary Recall Product Information," http://www.castleberrys.com/news_productrecall.asp (posted July 21, 2007); Centers for Disease Control and Prevention (CDC), "Recalls, Market Withdrawals, and Safety Alerts," http://www.fda.gov/opacom/7alerts.html (accessed October 16, 2009); Food Safety and Inspection Service, "FSIS Recalls," http://www.fsis.usda.gov/Fsis_Recalls/index.asp (accessed October 16, 2009); CDC, "Botulism Associated with Canned Chili Sauce, July-August 2007," http://www.cdc.gov/botulism/botulism.htm (updated August 24, 2007).

3. J. Barry et al., "Botulism in Injecting Drug Users, Dublin, Ireland, November–December 2008," *Eurosurveillance* 14, no. 1 (January 8, 2009).

4. Marler Clark LLP, "California Says Mexican Black Tar Heroin Use to Blame for Epidemic of Wound Botulism," http://www.botulismblog.com/2009/01/articles/botulism-watch/california-says-mexican-black-tar-heroin-use-to-blame-for-epidemic-of-wound-botulism (posted January 5, 2009).

5. Pritzker Law, "Home-Canned Beans Lead to Botulism in Ohio," http://food-poisoning.pritzkerlaw.com/archives/botulism-homecanned-beans-lead-to-botulism-in-ohio.html (posted November 3, 2008).

6. *The Seattle Times,* "3 in Spokane Sickened by Canned-bean Botulism," http://seattletimes.nwsource.com/html/local-news/2008796749_apwabotulismwarning.html (February 28, 2009).

7. CDC, "Surveillance for Foodborne Disease Outbreaks—United States, 2006," *Morbidity and Mortality Weekly Report* 58, no. 22 (June 12, 2009) :609–615.

Chapter 3

1. P. Stenmark et al., "Crystal Structure of Botulinum Neurotoxin Type A in Complex with the Cell Surface Co-Receptor GT1b—Insight into the Toxin–Neuron Interaction," *PLoS Pathogens* 4, no. 8, http://www.plospathogens.org/article/info:doi%2F10.1371%2Fjournal.ppat.1000129.

2. DOE/Brookhaven National Laboratory, "Drug Target For The Most Potent Botulinum Neurotoxin Determined," *Medical News Today,* http://www.medicalnewstoday.com/articles/105834.php (posted April 30, 2008).

3. DOE/Brookhaven National Laboratory, "Structure Of New Botulism Nerve Toxin Subtype Revealed," *ScienceDaily,* http://www.sciencedaily.com/releases/2008/12/081222163049.htm (posted January 2, 2009).

Chapter 5

1. S. S. Arnon et al., "Botulinum Toxin as a Biological Weapon: Medical and Public Health Management," *Journal of the American Medical Association* 8 (2001): 1059–1070; D. R. Franz et al., "Clinical Recognition and Management of Patients Exposed to Biological Warfare Agents," *Journal of the American Medical Association* 5 (1997): 399–411.

2. EyeMarker Systems, Inc., "EyeMarker RTD1000 Offers First Non-Invasive Detection Of Botulism," *Medical News Today,* http://www.medicalnewstoday.com/articles/133017.php (posted December 15, 2008).

Chapter 7

1. S. S. Arnon et al., "Human Botulism Immune Globulin for the Treatment of Infant Botulism," *New England Journal*

of Medicine 354, no. 5 (February 2, 2006): 462–71.

2. Cangene Corporation, "Cangene's heptavalent botulism antitoxin delivered and accepted into U.S. Strategic National Stockpile," news release, September 27, 2008.

Chapter 9

1. N. Singer, "So Botox Isn't Just Skin Deep" *The New York Times*, April 12, 2009.

2. Ibid.

3. S. Boyles, "Black Box Warning for Botox, FDA: Cosmetic Use Appears Safe" WebMD, April 30, 2009, http://www.webmed.com/skin-problems-and-treatments/news/20090430/black-box-warning-for-botox?page=2

Chapter 10

1. D. G. McNeil, "Botox Frees Muscles for Stroke Patients in the Know" *The New York Times*, March 24, 2009.

Glossary

aerobe—An organism that requires and utilizes oxygen in its cellular respiration.

amino acids—The building blocks of protein.

anaerobe—An organism that does not and cannot use oxygen in its cellular respiration. For some organisms, oxygen is lethal.

anaphylaxis—A severe form of allergic reaction.

antibiotic—A drug capable of killing bacteria. It is not useful in fighting viruses.

antibody—A chemical produced by the immune system. It is used to neutralize toxins.

antigen—A chemical that stimulates the production of antibodies (antibody generating).

antitoxin—A type of antibody that neutralizes poisons (toxins) released by organisms such as bacteria.

archae—A group of microorganisms that contains genetic information similar to the eukaryotes and also genetic information similar to bacteria. They live in extreme environments and are sometimes called "extremophiles."

bacillus—The term used with an uppercase "B" refers to a specific genus of bacteria that has a rod-like shape; when used with the lowercase "b" the term refers to the rod-like shape of many bacteria.

bioterrorism—Any actual or threatened use of microorganisms or their products (toxins) to cause death or disease in animals, humans, or plants.

botulism—An illness caused by a bacterium (*Clostridium botulinum*) that produces deadly protein toxins.

bubonic—The swelling of the lymph nodes.

clinical trials—Rigorous scientific evaluation of a procedure, device or drug(s) used for prevention, diagnosis, or treatment of a disease.

coccus—A bacterial cell that resembles a sphere.

debriding—Surgically removing the skin of an affected area to treat wound botulism.

DNA (deoxyribonucleic acid)—The molecule that represent the genetic information in all known organisms.

effector—An organ that becomes active when stimulated.

endospore—Survival structure produced by bacteria when it comes in contact with air.

enzyme—A protein that speeds up the rate of a biochemical reaction.

epidemic—A dramatic increase in the number of individuals showing the symptoms of a certain disease.

eukaryotic—A type of organism that contains one or more cells with a nucleus and other well-developed compartments known as organelles.

gastric lavage—Also known as pumping the stomach; the procedure involves placing a tube down the throat into the stomach so that the contents may be suctioned out for analysis or so that fluids may be pumped into the stomach.

genome—The total of all the genetic information in a cell or virus.

gram-negative bacteria—Bacteria that lose the color of the first or primary stain (crystal violet) and takes the color of the second or counterstain during the gram stain procedure. The organisms responsible for typhoid fever, cholera, and bubonic plague are gram-negative.

gram-positive bacteria—Bacteria that retain the color of the crystal violet stain during the gram stain procedure. The *C. botulinum* bacterium is gram-positive.

hypersensitivity reaction—A condition in which the immune system misidentifies a protein in an antitoxin preparation as a potentially harmful molecule and develops an immune response against it.

infant botulism—When a child contracts the disease produced by the bacterium *C. botulinum*; it is the most common form of the disease.

inhalation botulism—A form of botulism in which the bacterial toxin is inhaled into the lungs.

interneurons—Nerves found wthin the central nervous system; connect sensory and motor neurons.

intestinal colonization—A large number of botulism organisms growing and reproducing in the intestines.

intubation—An intervention for respiratory failure and paralysis that usually occurs with severe botulism. It requires that a tube be inserted through the nose or mouth into the trachea (windpipe) to provide an airway for oxygen.

mechanical ventilation—A potential intervention in the case of respiratory failure and the paralysis that usually occurs with severe botulism where a machine is used to assist breathing.

messenger RNA (mRNA)—One of three forms of RNA; carries a copy of the coded genetic information from the DNA molecule to the ribosomes.

mortality rate—The number of deaths in a given population during a given time period that are identified as being caused by a specific disease agent.

motor neuron—A nerve cell that controls and relays messages about movement.

nasogastric feeding—Intravenous fluids given through a tube inserted in the nose.

neuroglia—Glial cells; nervous tissue that nourishes and provides support for neurons.

neuron—Cells that send nerve signals between the parts of the nervous system.

organelles—Small structures in the cell that perform certain functions.

parasite—An organism or viral particle that invades and lives within another cell or organism (called the host). The parasite benefits from the relationship but the host is harmed or may be killed.

pathogen—An organism that causes disease in another organism.

peptidoglycan—A molecule that contains amino acids (the building blocks of proteins), and carbohydrates (including simple sugars like glucose). Bacterial cell walls are largely made of this molecule.

prokaryotic—Cells that lack membrane-enclosed organelles such as a nucleus.

proteolytic—Capable of breaking down proteins.

receptor-mediated endocytosis—The process by which a cell takes in other cells, particles, or molecules after attaching to specific protein receptor molecules in the host cell's membrane.

ribosome—Structures in both prokaryotic and eukaryotic cells that produce proteins.

riboswitch—RNA molecules that regulate gene action by attaching to the product of the gene's information and, thus, act as a control switch.

ribozyme—RNA molecule that acts like an enzyme.

RNA (ribonucleic acid)—A nucleic acid that occurs in three forms, each with a different function in the process of protein synthesis: ribosomal RNA (rRNA), messenger RNA (mRNA), and transfer RNA (tRNA).

sensory neuron—A nerve cell that takes messages from a sensory receptor to the central nervous system.

serum—The clear, light yellow-orange fluid left when the formed elements (cells) and the clotting factors are removed from blood.

shock—A condition that results from a rapid loss of fluid volume from the bloodstream thereby rapidly and dangerously causing a drop in blood pressure.

spirilli—Spiral-shaped bacteria.

synaptic vesicle—Encapsulated form in which a neurotransmitter is brought to a cell membrane for release from a nerve cell.

trachea—Also known as the windpipe in vertebrate organisms; a tube that runs from the larynx to the bronchi and is supported (held open) by a series of rings made of cartilage.

toxin—Poison produced by a disease-causing organism.

urticaria—Skin eruptions that are red, circular, itchy, and slightly raised above the skin level. This condition is a possible side effect from an antitoxin.

vaccine—A medication given to increase immunity to a specific disease.

weaponization—Creating mechanisms and procedures that increase the ability of an agent to cause infection or death.

wound botulism—Rare form of botulsim that occurs when endospores of *C. botulinum* enter under the skin through a cut or open sore.

Bibliography

Agres, T. "Companies on the Fence About Biodefense." *The Scientist* 18 (2004): 20.

Ahn-Yoon, S., and R. A. Durst. "Ganglioside-Liposome Immunoassay for the Detection of Botulinum Toxin." *Analytical and Bioanalytical Chemistry* 378 (2004): 68–75. In May, M., "Building a Better Biosensor." *The Scientist* 18 (2004): 36.

Anderson, M. "Studying Bioterrorism." *The Scientist.* Available online at http://www.biomedcentral.com/news/20040727/04.

Arnon, S. S., R. Schechter, T. V. Inglesby, et al. "Botulinum Toxin as a Biological Weapon: Medical and Public Health Management." *Journal of American Medical Association* 8 (2001): 1059–1070.

Biological Warfare Research in the United States; vol II. Archived at the U.S. Army Medical Research Institute of Infectious Diseases, Ft. Dedrick, Md.

Black, R. E., and R. A. Gunn. "Hypersensitivity Reactions Associated with Botulinal Antitoxin." *American Journal of Medicine* 69 (1980): 567–570.

Boyd, W., V. Stringer, and P. Williams. "Metal LC50 Values of Soil Nematode Compared to Earthworm Data," in *Environmental Toxicology and Risk Assessment, Science, Policy, and Standardization: Implications for Environmental Decisions.* Vol 10. West Conshohocken, Pa.: American Society for Testing and Materials, 2001.

Brochetti, D. "Can It Safely." *Centers for Disease Control and Prevention.* Available online at http://www.cdc.gov/nasd/docs/ d001201-d001300/d001284/d001284.html.

Bruhn, C. M. "Consumer Concerns: Motivating to Action." *Emerging Infectious Diseases* 3 (1997): 453–457.

Byrne, M. P., and L. A. Smith. "Development of Vaccines for Prevention of Botulism." *Biochimie* 9–10 (2000): 955–966.

Centers for Disease Control and Prevention (CDC). *Botulism in the United States, 1899–1996: Handbook for Epidemiologists, Clinicians, and Laboratory Workers.* Atlanta: Centers for Disease Control and Prevention, 1998.

CDC. "Botulism Outbreak Associated with Eating Fermented Food—Alaska, 2001." *Morbidity and Mortality Weekly Report* 50 (2001): 680–682.

CDC. "New Telephone Number to Report Botulism Cases and Request Antitoxin." *Morbidity and Mortality Weekly Report* 32 (2003): 774.

CDC. "Summary of Notifiable Diseases, United States, 2000." *Morbidity and Mortality Weekly Report* 53 (2002): 1–100.

CDC. "Summary of Notifiable Diseases—United States, 2001." *Morbidity and Mortality Weekly Report* 53 (2003): 1–108.

CDC. "Table I, Summary of Provisional Cases of Selected Notifiable Diseases, United States..." *Morbidity and Mortality Weekly Report* 37 (2004): 880–888.

CDC. "Wound Botulism—California 1995." *Morbidity and Mortality Weekly Report* 48 (1995): 889–892.

CDC/NIH. "Summary of Recommended Biosafety Levels (BSL) for Infectious Agents." *Research, Scholarship, and Creative Activity at the University of Michigan.* Available online at http://www.research.umich.edu/policies/um/committees/BRRC/BSLChartCDCNIH.html.

CHC Medical Library. "Botulism." *CHC Medical Library & Patient Education.* Available online at http://www.chclibrary.org/micromed/00040460.html.

Chin, J., S. S. Arnon, and T. F. Midura. "Food and Environmental Aspects of Infant Botulism in California." *Infectious Diseases Review* 4 (1979): 693–697.

"Clinical Studies: Testing New Medicines." *ClinicalStudyResults.org.* Available online at http://www.clinicalstudyresults.org/primers/testing_new_medicine.php.

Cochrane, R. C. *History of the Chemical Warfare Service in World War II (1 July 1940–15 August 1945).* Historical Section, Plans, Training, and Intelligence Division, Office of Chief, Chemical Corps, U.S. Army; November 1947.

Coffield, J. A., et al. "*In Vitro* Characterization of Botulinum Toxin Types A, C, and D Action on Human Tissues: Combined Electrophysiologic, Pharmacologic, and Molecular Biologic Approaches." *Journal of Pharmacology and Experimental Therapeutics* 280 (1997): 1489.

Council for Responsible Genetics. "Mistakes Happen: Accidents and Security Breaches at Biocontainment Laboratories." *Council for Responsible Genetics: Boston University Biodefense.* Available online at http://www.gene-watch.org/bubiodefense/pages/accidents.html.

Davidson, K. "'Star Trek' Device Can Test Water for Safety. Sandia Introduces 'MicroChemLab' to Foil Terrorists." *San Francisco Chronicle*, December 7, 2004, B-5.

Epel, D. "Common Synthetic Fragrances Harmful to Marine Life." *California Sea Grant Stories.* Available online at http://www-csgc.ucsd.edu/NEWSROOM/NEWSRELEASES/Fragrance_Epel.html.

EyePlastics. "Blepharospasm & Botox: How Botox Works." *EyePlastics.* Available online at http://www.eyeplastics.com/topics/botox/botox_mechanism.htm.

Feigin, R. D., and J. D. Cherry, eds. "Infant Botulism Treatment and Prevention Program." *Textbook of Pediatric Infectious Disease, 4th ed.* Philadelphia: W. B. Saunders Company, 1998.

Franz, D. R., P. B. Jahrling, A. M. Friedlander, et al. "Clinical Recognition and Management of Patients Exposed to Biological Warfare Agents." *Journal of American Medical Association* 5 (1997): 399–411.

Garrett, L. *Betrayal of Trust: The Collapse of Global Public Health.* New York: Hyperion Books, 2000.

Gendreau, M. "Gastric Lavage." *Clinical Toxicology Review* 35 (1997): 711–719.

Graham, S. "Nanoparticles Enable Speedy *E. coli* Detection." *Scientific American,* October 12, 2004.

Giladi, N. "The Mechanism of Action of Botulinum Toxin Type A in Focal Dystonia Is Most Probably Through Its Dual Effect on Efferent (Motor) and Afferent Pathways at the Injected Site." *Journal of Neurological Science* 2 (1997): 132–135.

Gilchrist, M. J. R. "The Progress, Priorities, and Concerns of Public Health Laboratories." *Association of Public Health Laboratories.* Available online at http://www.aphl.org/docs/Advocacy/Testimonies/IOMBioterrorism11-28-01.pdf.

Greater Oncology Today. "Expanded Uses for Botulinum Toxin Benefit Head and Neck Patients." *GBMC HealthCare.* Available online at http://www.gbmc.org/publications/oncologytodayfall03/toxin.

Hamann, B. *Disease: Identification, Prevention, and Control.* St. Louis, Mo.: Mosby-Year Book, Inc., 1994.

Hatheway, C. L. "Botulism: The Present Status of the Disease." *Current Topics in Microbiology and Immunology* 195 (1995): 55–75.

Hatheway, C. L., J. D. Snyder, J. E. Seals, et al. "Antitoxin Levels in Botulism Patients Treated with Trivalent Equine Botulinum Antitoxin to Toxin Types A, B, and E." *The Journal of Infectious Diseases* 1 (1984): 407–412.

Health Encyclopedia. "Causes of Infant Botulism." *drkoop.com.* Available online at http://drkoop.com/encyclopedia/93/461. html#causes.

Health Physics Society. "Food Irradiation." *University of Michigan.* Available online at http://www.umich.edu/~radinfo/intro duction/food.htm.

Health Protection Agency. "Emergent BioSolutions and HPA Announce Botulinum Vaccine Collaboration." *Health Protection Agency.* Available online at http://www.hpa.org.uk/hpa/ news/articles/press_releases/2005/050114_botulinum.htm.

Hill, E. V. "Botulism." Summary Report on B.W. Investigations. Memorandum to Alden C. Waitt, Chief Chemical Corps, United States Army, December 12, 1947; tab D. Archived at the U.S. Library of Congress.

Holder, D. "Anti-Botulism Vaccine Is Goal." *Research Nebraska* 8 (1997): 10–11.

"Home-Canned Enterotoxin." CD Summary, Volume 46, No. 12, Center for Disease Prevention & Epidemiology, Oregon Health Division, June 10, 1997.

Homecanning.com. "Basics: Step-by-Step." *homecanning.com.* Available online at http://www.homecanning.com/usa/ALStep ByStep.asp.

IGEN. "IGEN to Supply Botulinum Toxin Tests to USDA's ISIS." *Infection Control Today.* Available online at http://www.infec tioncontroltoday.com/hotnews/34h2271710.html?wts=200501 15011801&hc=112&req=Botulinum+and+toxin+and+tests.

International Commission on Microbiological Specifications for Foods. "*Clostridium botulinum.*" *Micro-organisms in Foods 5: Characteristics of Microbial Pathogens.* New York: Blackie Academic & Professional, 1996.

Jankovic, J. and M. F. Brin. "Therapeutic Uses of Botulinum Toxin." *New England Journal of Medicine* 324 (1991): 1186.

Johansson, J., P. Mandin, A. Renzoni, C. Chiaruttini, M. Springer, and P. Cossart. "An RNA Thermosensor Controls Expression of Virulence Genes in *Listeria monocytogenes.*" *Cell* 110 (2002): 551–561.

Kalluri, P., C. Crowe, M. Reller, L. Gaul, J. Hayslett, S. Barth, S. Eliasberg, et al. "An Outbreak of Foodborne Botulism Associated with Food Sold at a Salvage Store in Texas." *Clinical Infecioust Diseases* 11 (2003): 1490–1495.

Kao, I., D. B. Drachman, and D. L. Price. "Botulinum Toxin: Mechanism of Presynaptic Blockade." *Science* 4259 (1976): 1256–1258.

Kendall, P. "Botulism." *Colorado State University Cooperative Extension.* Available online at http://www.ext.colostate.edu/pubs/foodnut/09305.html.

Kessler, K. R., and R. Benecke. "Botulinum Toxin: From Poison to Remedy." *Neurotoxicology* 3 (1997): 761–770.

Kittredge, C. "*The Scientist*: BU BSL-4 Lab Faces More Scrutiny." *BioMed Central.* Available online at http://www.biomedcentral.com/news/20050124/02.

Kiyatkin, N., A. B. Maksymowych, and L. L. Simpson. "Induction of an Immune Response by Oral Administration of Recombinant Botulinum Toxin." *Infection and Immunity* 65 (1997): 4586.

Koirala, J., and S. Basnet. "Botulism, Botulinum Toxin, and Bioterrorism: Review and Update." *Infections in Medicine* 6 (2004): 284–290.

Kortepeter, M. M., G. Christopher, T. Cieslak, et al. "Bululinum." In *USAMRIID's Medical Management of Biological Casualties Handbook.* 4th ed. Fort Dedrick, Md.: US Army Medical Research Institute of Infectious Diseases; 2001: 70–75.

Ludlow, C. L. "Treatment of Speech and Voice Disorders with Botulinum Toxin." *Journal of American Medical Association* 264 (1990): 2671.

MacDonald, K. L., R. F. Spengler, C. L. Hatheway, N. T. Hargrett, and M. L. Cohen. "Type A Botulism from Sautéed Onions. Clinical and Epidemiologic Observations." *Journal of the American Medical Association* 9 (1985): 1275–1278.

Mellors, R. C. "Hypersensitivity Reactions: Tissue Injury Initiated by Immune Responses." *Weill Medical College of Cornell University.* Available online at http://edcenter.med.cornell.edu/CUMC_PathNotes/Immunopathology/Immuno_02.html.

Mims, C. A. *The Pathogenesis of Infectious Disease.* New York: Academic Press, 1977.

Mironov, A., I. Gusarov, R. Rafikov, L. Lopez, K. Shatalin, R. A. Kreneva, D. A. Perumov, and E. Nudler. "Sensing Small Molecules by Nascent RNA: A Mechanism to Control Transcription in Bacteria." *Cell* 111 (2002): 747–756.

Montecucco, C., and G. Schiavo. "Mechanism of Action of Tetanus and Botulinum Neurotoxins." *Molecular Microbiology* 1 (1994): 1–8.

Morrison, J. L. "Botulinum Toxin as a Disease Agent." *Biohazard News.* Available online at http://www.biohazardnews.net/agent_botox.shtml.

Münchau, A., and K. P. Bhatia. "Clinical Review: Uses of Botulinum Toxin in Medicine Today." *bmj.com: The General Medical Journal Website.* Available online at http://bmj.bmjjournals.com/cgi/content/full/320/7228/161.

Nahvi A., N. Sudarsan, M. Ebert, X. Zou, K. Brown, and R. R. Breaker. "Genetic Control by a Metabolite Binding mRNA." *Journal of Biological Chemistry* 9 (2002): 1043–1049.

National Multiple Sclerosis Society. "The Uses of Botulinum Toxin in Multiple Sclerosis." *National Multiple Sclerosis Society.* Available online at http://www.nationalmssociety.org/Clinup-Botox.asp.

Nevas, M., M. Lindstrom, A. Virtanen, S. Hielm, M. Kuusi, S. S. Arnon, E. Vuori, and H. Korkeala. "Infant Botulism Acquired from Household Dust Presenting as Sudden Infant Death Syndrome." *Journal of Clinical Microbiology* 1 (2005): 511–513.

NIAID. "Botulism: August 2003." *National Institute of Allergy and Infectious Diseases/National Institutes of Health.* Available online at http://www.niaid.nih.gov/Publications/botulism.htm.

Ohio State University Extension. "Ensuring Safe Food—A HACCP-Based Plan for Ensuring Food Safety in Retail Establishments: Bulletin 901." *Ohio State University Ohioline.* Available online at http://ohioline.osu.edu/b901/index.html.

Olson, K. B. "*Aum Shinrikyo*: Once and Future Threat?" *Emerging Infectious Diseases* 5 (1999): 513–516.

Pasricha, P. J., et al. "Intrasphincteric Botulinum Toxin for the Treatment of Achalasia." *New England Journal of Medicine* 332 (1995): 774.

Passaro, D. J., et al. "Wound Botulism Associated with Black Tar Heroin Among Injecting Drug Users." *Journal of American Medical Association* 11 (1998): 859–863.

"Possession, Use, and Transfer of Select Agents and Toxins." Interim Final Rule. *Federal Register,* December 13, 2002.

The Regal Swan. "Success in Battle Against Botulism in Swans." *The Royal Windsor Website.* Available online at http://www.thamesweb.co.uk/swans/swan_project2002.html.

RnCeus.com. "Botulism." *RnCeus.com.* Available online at http://www.rnceus.com/biot/botul.html.

Sandia National Laboratories. "Sandia National Laboratories Presents Fully Integrated Lab-on-a-Chip Development." *Sandia National Laboratories.* Available online at http://www.sandia.gov/media/NewsRel/NR2000/labchip.htm.

Sanford, M. T. "Infant Botulism and Honey." *University of Florida: Institute of Food and Agricultural Services Extension.* Available online at http://edis.ifas.ufl.edu/scripts/htmlgen.exe?DOCUMENT_AA142.

Schantz, E. J. and E. A. Johnson. "Properties and Use of Botulinum Toxin and Other Microbial Neurotoxins in Medicine." *Clinical Microbiology Reviews* 1 (1992): 80–99.

Schwartz, M. "Common Household Fragrances May Be Harming Aquatic Wildlife." *Medical News Today.* Available online at http://www.medicalnewstoday.com/medicalnews.php?newsid=15643.

Scott, A. B. "Botulinum Toxin Injection into Extraocular Muscles as an Alternative to Strabismus Surgery." *Journal of Pediatric Opthalmology & Strabismus* 17 (1980): 21.

Seals, J. E., J. D. Snyder, T. A. Edell, C. L. Hatheway, C. J. Johnson, R. C. Swanson, and J. M. Hugh. "Restaurant-Associated Type A Botulism: Transmission by Potato Salad." *American Journal of Epidemiology* 113 (1981): 436–444

Shaffer, N., R. B. Wainwright, J. P. Middaugh, and R. V. Tauxe. "Botulism Among Alaska Natives. The Role of Changing Food

Preparation and Consumption Practices." *Western Journal of Medicine* 4 (1990): 390–393.

Shen, W. P., N. Felsing, D. Lang, et al. "Development of Infant Botulism in a 3-Year-old Female with Neuroblastoma Following Autologous Bone Marrow Transplantation: Potential Use of Human Botulism Immune Globulin." *Bone Marrow Transplantation* 13 (1994): 345–347.

Simpson, L. L. "Botulinum Toxin: Potent Poison, Potent Medicine." *Hospital Practice: Advances in Medicine for Primary Care Physicians.* Available online at http://www.hosppract.com/issues/1999/04/simpson.htm.

Solomon, H. M., and T. Lilly, Jr. "*Clostridium botulinum.*" In Jackson, G. H., R. I. Merker, and R. Bandler, project coordinators. *Bacteriological Analytical Manual Online.* Washington, D.C.: FDA CFSAN, January 2001.

South Carolina Department of Health and Environmental Control. "South Carolina Health Alert Network: Botulism." *South Carolina Department of Health and Environmental Control.* Available online at http://www.scdhec.gov/health/disease/han/botulism.htm.

Spika, J. S., et al. "Risk Factors for Infant Botulism in the United States." *American Journal of Diseases of Children* 143 (1989): 828–832.

Sprague, L. A., and W. A. Battaglin. "Wastewater Chemicals in Colorado's Streams and Ground Water." (2005) U.S. Geological Survey Fact Sheet 2004–3127, p. 4.

Subramaniam E., D. Kumaran, and S. Swaminathan. "A Novel Mechanism for *Clostridium botulinum* Neurotoxin Inhibition." *Biochemistry* 31 (2002) 9795–9802.

Suen C., C. L. Hatheway, A. G. Steigerwalt, and D. J. Brenner. "Genetic Confirmation of Identities of Neurotoxigenic *Clostridium baratii* and *Clostridium butyricum* Implicated as Agents of Infant Botulism." *Journal of Clinical Microbiology* 10 (1988): 2191–2192.

Swaddiwudhipong, W., and P. Wongwatcharapaiboon. "Foodborne Botulism Outbreaks Following Consumption of Home-Canned Bamboo Shoots in Northern Thailand." *Journal of the Medical Association of Thailand* 9 (2000): 1021-1-25.

Tacket, C. O., W. X. Shandera, J. M. Mann, et al. "Equine Antitoxin Use and Other Factors That Predict Outcome in Type A

Foodborne Botulism." *American Journal of Medicine* 76 (1984): 794–798.

Tammemagi, L., and K. M. Grant. "Vaccination in the Control of Bovine Botulism in Queensland." *Australian Veterinarian Journal* 9 (1967): 368–372.

Therapeutics and Technology Assessment Subcommittee, American Academy of Neurology. "Training Guidelines for the Use of Botulinum Toxin for the Treatment of Neurologic Disorders." *Neurology* 44 (1994): 2401.

Therre, H. "Botulism in the European Union." *Eurosurveillance* 4 (1999): 2–7.

Townes, J. M., P. R. Cieslak, C. L. Hatheway, H. M. Solomon, J. T. Holloway, M. P. Baker, C. F. Keller, L. M. McCroskey, and P. M. Griffin, "An Outbreak of Type A Botulism Associated with a Commercial Cheese Sauce." *Annals of Internal Medicine* 125 (1996): 558–563.

Travis, J. "Quite a Switch: Bacteria and Perhaps Other Life Forms Use RNA as Environmental Sensors." *Science News* 165 (2004): 232.

Tucker, J. B., ed. *Toxic Terror: Assessing the Terrorist Use of Chemical and Biological Weapons.* Cambridge, Mass.: MIT Press, 2000.

United Nations Security Council. *Tenth Report of the Executive Chairman of the Special Commission Established by the Secretary-General Pursuant to Paragraph 9(b)(I) of Security Council Resolution 687 (1991), and Paragraph 3 of Resolution 699 (1991) on the Activities of the Special Commission.* New York: United Nations Security Council, 1995.

University of Miami. "Education Procedures: Myobloc—Mode of Action." *University of Miami Cosmetic Center.* Available online at http://www.derm.net/my_mode_of_action.shtml.

Urticaria.com. "What Is Urticaria?" *Urticaria.com.* Available online at http://www.urticaria.com/what.htm.

USAMRIID. "Home Page." *U.S. Army Medical Research Institute of Infectious Diseases.* Available online at http://www.usamriid.army.mil/index.htm.

U.S. Department of Health and Human Services, National Institutes of Health, Publication No. 01-4730, April 2001.

Washington University in St. Louis. "Botulism." *Department of Neurology Website.* Available online at http://www.neuro.wustl.edu/neuromuscular/nother/bot.htm.

West Virginia Infectious Disease Epidemiology Program. "Protocol: Botulism Surveillance & Response." *West Virginia Department of Health & Human Services.* Available online at http://www.wvdhhr.org/idep/botulism_protocol.htm.

Williamson, D. M., R. B. Gravani, and H. T. Lawless. "Correlating Food Safety Knowledge with Home Food-Preparation Practices." *Food Technology* 46 (1992): 94–100.

Winkler, W., A. Nahvi, and R. R. Breaker. "Thiamine Derivatives Bind Messenger RNAs Directly to Regulate Bacterial Gene Expression." *Nature* 419 (2002): 952–956.

Winkler W., S. Cohen-Chalamish, and R. R. Breaker. "An mRNA Structure That Controls Gene Expression by Binding FMN." *Proceedings of the National Academy of Sciences* 99 (2002): 15908–15913.

W. M. Keck Foundation Biotechnology Resource Laboratory. "Affymetrix Genechip Technology Overview." *W. M. Keck Foundation Biotechnology Resource Laboratory.* Available online at http://info.med.yale.edu/wmkeck/affymetrix/technology.htm#technology.

WuDunn, S., J. Miller, and W. J. Broad. "How Japan Germ Terror Alerted the World." *New York Times,* May 26, 1998, A1, A10.

Zhang, R., T. Pappas, J. L. Brace, P. C. Miller, T. Oulmassov, J. M. Molyneaux, J. C. Anderson, et al. "Structure of a Bacterial Quorum-sensing Transcription Factor Complexed with Pheromone and DNA." *Nature* 417 (2002): 971–974.

Zhao, L., T. J. Montville, and D. W. Schaffner. "Computer Simulation of *Clostridium botulinum* Strain 56A Behavior at Low Spore Concentrations." *Applied and Environmental Microbiology* 69 (2003): 845–851.

Zhao, L., T. J. Montville, and D. W. Schaffner. "Effect of Inoculum Size on Maximum Growth Rate, Lag Time and Maximum Percent Growth of *Clostridium botulinum* at Varying pH and Salt Concentration." *Journal of Food Microbiology and Safety.* Volume 24 (2000):309-314.

Zilinskas, R. A. "Iraq's Biological Weapons: The Past as Future?" *Journal of American Medical Association* 278 (1997): 418–424.

Further Resources

Books and Articles

Alibek, K. and S. Handleman. *Biohazard*. New York: Random House, 1999.

Botox Debate. "Medical Uses for Botox." *Botox Debate*. Available online at http://www.botox-debate.com/medical-uses.php.

CIDRAP. "Bioterrorism: Botulism." *Center for Infectious Disease Research & Policy: University of Minnesota*. Available online at http://www.cidrap.umn.edu/cidrap/content/bt/botulism/index.html.

Greenfield, R. A., and M. S. Bronze. "Prevention and Treatment of Bacterial Diseases Caused by Bacterial Bioterrorism Threat Agents." *Drug Discovery Today* 19 (2003): 881–888.

Jankovic, J., and M. Hallett, eds. *Therapy with Botulinum Toxin*. New York: Marcel Dekker, 1994.

National Institutes of Health. "Consensus Conference: Clinical Use of Botulinum Toxin." *Connecticut Medicine* 55 (1991): 471.

Patocka, J., and M. Splino, "Botulinum Toxin: From Poison to Medicinal Agent." *The Applied Science and Analysis Newsletter,* February 2002.

Shapiro, R. L., C. Hatheway, and D. L. Swerdlow. "Botulism in the United States: A Clinical and Epidemiologic Review." *Annals of Internal Medicine* 129 (1998): 221–228.

Simpson, L. L. "Botulinum Toxin: A Deadly Poison Sheds Its Negative Image." *Annals of Internal Medicine* 125 (1996): 616.

Southern Illinois University, School of Medicine. "Botulism: Toxicology, Clinical Presentation, and Management." *Department of Internal Medicine Website*. Available online at http://www.siumed.edu/medicine/id/current/botulism.htm.

World Health Organization. "Botulism Fact Sheet No 270, Revised August 2002." *World Health Organization*. Available online at http://www.who.int/mediacentre/factsheets/who270/en/.

Web Sites

A Short History of Botulism–Odorless, Tasteless, But Certainly Not Harmless
http://iaith.tapetrade.net/botulism

CBRNE–Botulism (Overview)
http://www.emedicine.com/EMERG/topic64.htm

Botulism Surveillance and Response
http://www.wvdhhr.org/idep/botulism_protocol.htm

Infant Botulism Treatment and Prevention Program
http://www.dhs.ca.gov/ps/dcdc/InfantBot/ibtindex.htm

Wound Botulism–California, 1995
http://www.dhs.ca.gov/ps/dcdc/cm/951001cm.htm

Clemson University Fact Sheet
http://hgic.clemson.edu/
factsheets/HGIC3680.htm

Safety Precautions for Botulism Casualties
http://www.cbwinfo.com/Biological/Pathogens/CBo.html

World Heath Organization, Fact Sheet 270
http://www.who.int/mediacentre/factsheets/who270/en/

National Disease Surveillance Center
http://www.ndsc.ie/DiseaseTopicsA-Z/Botulism/

The National Institute of Allergy and Infectious Diseases
(NIAID)
http://www.niaid.nih.gov/
publications/botulism.htm

Index

acetylcholine, 59, 66–68
acidity
  of food, 20, 22, 25, 83, 86, 87–88
  of soil, 103–106
acute inflammatory demyelinating polyneuropathy. *See* Guillain-Barré Syndrome
adult infectious botulism, 14
aerobe/aerobic, 32
aerosolization, 14–15, 50
Affymetrix, Inc., 107
Agricultural Research Service Western Regional Research Center, 47
Agriculture Department, U.S., 23, 47, 110–111
A-Hold Corporation, 26
airtight containers, 83–85
Alaska, 9–10, 58, 75, 85
alewife, 24
Allergan, 102
altitude, 103–106
American Chemical Society, 107
American College of Physicians, 52
amino acid, 31, 34
aminoglycosides, 53, 74
anaerobe, 28, 30, 32, 83
anaphylaxis, 74, 75, 76, 79, 119
Animal Kingdom, 28
animals, toxins in, 38, 39
animal vaccines, 115–116, 119
anthrax, 94
antibiotic, 94
antibody(ies)
  in infant botulism treatment, 73–74
  monoclonal, 48
  in mouse test, 57–58
antigens, 76
anti-infective drugs, 6–7
antitoxin, 46, 74–81
  acquisition/availability of, 75, 81, 82–83, 118
  definition of, 74
  enhanced, research on, 96
  half-life of, 76
  hypersensitivity to, 74, 75, 76–79
  problems with, 75–79
  skin (scratch) test for, 76–77
aptamers, 112
Archae (Archaebacteria), 30–31
Arnon, Stephen S., 17
Ascher, Michael S., 58
Aum Shinrikyo, 92–93
autonomic nervous system, 62, 63, 64
autopsy specimens, 51

BabyBig, 73–74
bacillus, 32
Bacillus, 33, 34
bacteria, 28–40
  classification of, 28–31
  Gram stain of, 31, 32
  shape of, 32
  structure of, 31–32
Bacteria Domain, 31
Bacteria Kingdom, 28–31
BAT. *See* antitoxin
Battaglin, Bill, 103
belladonna toxicity, 53
BIG, 80
BIG-IV, 73–74
bilateral attack, 54, 69
Biodefense Microarray Test, 107–109
Biological and Toxin Weapons Convention (1972), 93
Biosafety Guideline: Biosafety in Microbiological and Biomedical Laboratories, 97
biosafety levels (BSLs), 97–101
bioterrorism, 8, 14–15, 40, 92–101
  CDC categories of agents, 94–95
  CDC criteria for agents, 94
  definition of, 14, 92
  history of, 92–96
  Laboratory Response Network and, 96–101
  Project Bioshield and, 113–114
  study of, 41–42
birds, 12, 17, 19, 115–116
black box label, for Botox, 102
black tar heroin, 18, 24, 89
blepharospasm, 60
blood-brain barrier, 69
boiling water *vs.* pressure cooking, 86–88
Bolthouse Farms, 21–22
Bon Vivant incident, 11, 20
Boston, 101
Botox, 60–61, 102–103, 115
botulinum toxin. *See* toxin(s)
botulism. *See also specific entries*
  bioterrorism potential of, 8, 14–15, 40, 92–101
  cases in U.S., 1994-2004, 93
  causative agent of, 8, 9
  causes of, 19–21, 28–40
  concerns for future, 92–106
  diagnosis of, 49–58, 96, 110–112
  geographic distribution of, 9–10, 13, 14
  hopes for future, 92, 107–119
  incidence of, 8–9, 15, 82, 92
  mortality rate from, 72
  prevention of, 82–91
  recent cases of, 21–27
  symptoms of, 69
  transmission of, 41–49
  treatment of, 46, 71–81
  types of, 8–15
botulism immune globulin (BIG), 73–74, 80
Breaker, Ronald, 112
breathing interventions, 71–72, 81
Brenner, Sydney, 109
Brin, Mitchell F., 102
Brock, Thomas, 30

Brookhaven National Laboratory, 39–40, 114
Bush, George W., 113

Caenorhabditis, 109
California, 17, 24, 75, 89, 104–105
California Sea Grant program, 104–105
Calumet, Lake, 33
Cambridge Biostability, 81, 118
Cangene Corporation, 81, 118
canned foods
    altitude and, 106
    boiling water *vs.* pressure cooking, 86–88
    safety for, 82, 85–88
    transmission via foods in, 20–25, 25, 43–46,
        56, 70
carrot juice, 21–22
Carruthers, Jean, 60
Castleberry Food Company, 23
CAT. *See* computed tomography
causative agent, 8, 9. *See also Clostridium
        botulinum*
CDC. *See* Centers for Disease Control and
        Prevention
cell(s)
    communication of, 37
    eukaryotic, 28–30
    nervous system, 63–65
    prokaryotic, 30
Center for Food Safety (UGA), 110
Centers for Disease Control and Prevention (CDC)
    antitoxin from, 75, 82–83
    biosafety guidelines of, 97
    bioterrorism categories and criteria of, 94–95
    National Center for Zoonotic, Vector-Borne,
        and Enteric Disease, 18
    national laboratory of, 97
    reports to/data of, 24, 27, 46, 82, 92
    testing research of, 96
central nervous system (CNS), 59–63
cerebrospinal fluid (CSF), 54, 55
cervical dystonia, 60
chemicals, in environment, 103–106
Chicago, 33
chili, 23, 92
cholera, 94
classification
    Domains, 31
    Kingdoms, 28–31
clindamycin, contraindication to, 74
clinical trials, 78, 79–81, 118
Clostridium, 33, 34
Clostridium argentinense, 37
Clostridium baratii, 37
Clostridium botulinum, 8, 9
    characteristics of, 32
    detection of, 46–48, 57–58, 96, 107–113
    dormant state of, 33, 36–37
    genetics/genome of, 95

Gram stain of, 31
identification of, 19
neurotoxins of, 9–10, 12, 37–40
quorum sensing by, 37
Clostridium butyricum, 37
CNS. *See* central nervous system
coccus (cocci), 32
Cochran, Grace Wallace, 11
Cochran, Samuel, Jr., 11
Colorado, 26, 103–106
communicable diseases, 6–7
computed tomography (CT or CAT), 54
cooking temperature, 28, 83, 84
Cornell University, 111
cosmetic use, 59, 102–103, 115
cranial nerves, 54, 69–70
crossed eyes, 60
CSF. *See* cerebrospinal fluid
CT. *See* computed tomography

debriding/debridement, 74
Defense Department, U.S., 39, 96
Defense Threat Reduction Agency, 39
deoxyribonucleic acid (DNA), 107–109, 112
Desulfotomaculum, 34
diagnosis, 49–58
    collecting samples for, 49–50, 51
    differential, 52, 53, 70
    rapid, non-invasive, 58
    tests for, 54–58, 96, 110–112
differential diagnosis, 52, 53, 70
disease, germ theory of, 29
DNA, 112
DNA fingerprinting, 107–109
Domains, 31
dormant state, 33, 36–37
Dublin, Ireland, 24
Durst, Richard, 111
DynPort Vaccine Company, 81, 118
Dysport, 102–103

E. (Escherichia) coli, 111
E. coli O157:H7, 46
ecotoxicology, 104
education, public, 82–83, 90, 119
effector, 64–65
electrochemiluminescence, 110–111
electromyogram (EMG), 56–57
Emergent BioSolutions, 118
emerging infections, 6
EMG. *See* electromyogram
endocytosis, receptor-mediated, 69
endopeptidase, 68
endospores, 33–37
    formation of, 28, 34, 35, 36
    functions of, 34
    geographic distribution of, 10
    germination in food, 83–85

medically significant, 34
resistant properties of, 33–34
enema, 51, 72
Energy Department, U.S., 39–40, 96, 107
environmental sample, 51
enzyme, 59, 68
Epel, David, 104, 105
epidemics, 17
Ermengem, Emile van, 19
Eukarya Domain, 31
eukaryotic cells, 28–30
extraction techniques, 47
extremophiles, 30
EyeMarker RTD 1000, 58
eye twitching, 60

FBB. *See* foodborne botulism
FBDOs. *See* foodborne disease outbreaks
FBDSS. *See* Foodborne Disease Outbreak
    Surveillance System
FDA. *See* Food and Drug Administration
flaccid paralysis, 10, 12, 17, 54
Florida, 21–22, 24, 111, 115–116
Food and Drug Administration (FDA), 11,
    79–80, 97, 102, 113
foodborne botulism (FBB), 8, 11
    A-Hold Corporation, 26
    Bolthouse Farms, 21–22
    Bon Vivant, 11, 20
    Castleberry, 23
    environmental factors in, 83, 84, 103–106
    foods associated with, 19–21, 44, 45
    garlic-in-oil, 26–27, 44
    history of, 16–19
    identifying sources of, 46–48, 109
    incidence of, 8–9, 15, 82, 92
    in Poland, 83, 86
    prevention of, 83–88, 90–91
    Stonewall Kitchen, 25–26
    toxin A and, 38–39
    transmission of, 41–46
    treatment of, 71–81
Foodborne Contaminants Research Unit, 47
foodborne disease outbreaks (FBDOs), 27
Foodborne Disease Outbreak Surveillance
    System (FBDSS), 27
foodborne illnesses, 8. *See also* foodborne
    botulism (FBB)
FOODPAC. *See* Food Processing Advisory Council
Food Processing Advisory Council (FOODPAC),
    110
food safety, 11, 20–21, 82, 85–88, 90–91, 106
Food Safety and Inspection Service (FSIS), 23,
    110–111
Fort Dedrick, Maryland, 97, 101
FSIS. *See* Food Safety and Inspection Service
Fungi Kingdom, 28

garlic-in-oil, 26–27, 44
gaspereaux (alewife), 24
gastric lavage, 72
gastric specimen, 51
GBS. *See* Guillain-Barré Syndrome
genetically modified organisms (GMOs), 47
genetics, of *Clostridium botulinum*, 95
genome, 34, 95
genomics, 95
geographic distribution, 9–10, 13, 14
George Mason University, 41–42
Georgetown University, 41–42
Georgia, 21–22, 109–110
Georgia Tech, 110
germination, 83–85
Germ Theory of Disease, 29
glial cells, 64, 66
GMOs. *See* genetically modified organisms
Gram-negative bacteria, 32
Gram-positive bacteria, 32
Gram stain, 31, 32
Great Britain, 118
Guillain-Barré Syndrome (GBS), 52, 53, 57, 70

Hazard Analysis and Critical Control Points
    (HACCP), 11, 20–21
headache, 60–61
head-up position, 71, 72, 73, 81
Health and Human Services Department, U.S., 95
Health Protection Agency (HPA, Great Britain), 118
heat pasteurization, 86
heptavalent antitoxin, 76, 80
heroin-related botulism, 18, 24, 89
history
    of bioterrorism, 92–96
    of botulism, 16–19
hives, 76
home canning
    altitude and, 106
    boiling water *vs.* pressure cooking, 86–88
    safety in, 82, 85–88
    transmission via foods in, 20–21, 22, 25,
        43–46, 56, 70
Homeland Security, Department of, 118
Homeland Security Institute, 42
Homeland Security Program, 111
honey, 12, 44, 45, 88–89
horse serum, 74
Horvitz, H. Robert, 109
hot dogs, 23
HPA. *See* Health Protection Agency
Huston, Roger, 95
hypersensitivity, 74, 75, 76–79, 119
hypersensitivity reaction, 77–79

IB. *See* infant botulism
IGEN International, Inc., 110–111

immune globulin, botulism, 73–74, 80
incidence, 8–9, 15, 82, 92
IND. *See* investigational new drug
infant botulism (IB), 8, 12
   California, 1976, 17
   flaccid paralysis with, 10, 17
   geographic distribution of, 13
   honey and, 12, 45, 88–89
   incidence of, 8–9, 15, 82
   prevention of, 88–89
   treatment of, 73–74, 75
infection, emerging or reemerging, 6
inhalation botulism, 15
inhibitor, of toxin, 39, 114
interneurons, 64
intestinal colonization, 12–14
intestinal fluid, 51
intubation, 71
investigational new drug (IND), 75
investigational use, 60–61
Iraq, 14, 93–94

Jafri, Kamran, 102
Japan, 14, 92–93, 113
juices, 21–22

Kerner, Justinus, 16–17
Kerner's Disease, 17
Kingdoms, 28–31
Koch, Robert, 28, 29
Koch's Postulates, 29

laboratories
   biosafety levels for, 97–101
   incidents at, 101
   national, 96, 97, 101
   recommendations for, 100
   reference, 96, 101
   sentinel, 96, 98–100
Laboratory Response Network (LRN), 96–101
Lambert-Eaton syndrome, 53
Landry's ascending paralysis. *See* Guillain-Barré
      Syndrome
laxatives, 72–73
lazy eye, 60
limberneck, in birds, 12, 17
Low-Acid Canned Food Regulations, 20
Luckenbach, Till, 105
lumbar puncture, 54, 55

Maryland, 97, 101, 118
Massachusetts, 101
McDonald, Paul, 11
Meagher, Mike, 117–118
mechanical ventilation, 71–72, 81
medical uses, of toxin, 59, 60–61, 102–103, 115
messenger RNA (mRNA), 112

MG. *See* myasthenia gravis
microarray testing, 107–109, 119
microbial genomics, 95
MicroChemLab, 107, 108
migraine, 60–61
Minton, Nigel, 95
molecular biology, 47
Monera. *See* Bacteria Kingdom
monoclonal antibodies, 48
Moore & Company, 11
mortality rate, 72
motor neurons, 64
mouse test, 56, 57
mRNA, 112
multiple sclerosis, 61
muscle contraction, 66–68
myasthenia gravis (MG), 52, 53, 56–57, 70
Myobloc, 60, 102–103

NACMCF. *See* National Advisory Committee on
      Microbiological Criteria for Food
nanoparticle, 111
nasal swab, 51
Nataro, James, 118
National Advisory Committee on
      Microbiological Criteria for Food
      (NACMCF), 20
National Center for Biodefense, 42
National Center for Zoonotic, Vector-Borne,
      and Enteric Disease (ZVED), 18
National Conference of Interstate Milk
      Shipment, 21
National Conference on Food Protection, 20
National Institute of Allergy and Infectious
      Diseases (NIAID), 95–96, 114
National Institutes of Health (NIH), 40, 95, 97, 113
national laboratories, 96, 97, 101
nematodes, for chemical testing, 109–110
nerves, affected by toxins, 54, 69–70
nervous system, 59–70
   botulinum toxin and, 68–70
   cells of, 63–65
   divisions of, 59–63
   functions of, 63
nettle rash, 76
neuroglia, 64, 66
neurons, 63–65
neurotoxins, 9–10, 12, 37–40. *See also specific toxins*
New York, 19, 89
NIAID. *See* National Institute of Allergy and
      Infectious Diseases
NIH. *See* National Institutes of Health

Office of Basic Energy Sciences, 39
Ontario, Canada, 22
organelles, 29–30
Origen technology, 110–111

pandemics, 6
paralysis
  differential diagnosis of, 52, 53, 70
  flaccid, 10, 12, 17, 54
  interventions for, 71–72, 81
parasites, 8
parasympathetic nervous system, 62, 63, 64
Passaro, Doug, 89
Pasteur, Louis, 29
pasteurization, 86
pathogens, 8
PCR. *See* polymerase chain reaction
PCT. *See* pressure cycling technology
Peck, M., 95
pentavalent botulinum toxoid, 75–76
pentavalent vaccine, 117, 118
peptidoglycan, 31–32
peripheral nervous system (PNS), 59–63
Pillsbury, 20
plague, 94
Plant Kingdom, 28
PNS. *See* peripheral nervous system
Poland, 83, 86
poliomyelitis, 53
polymerase chain reaction (PCR), 96
polyvalent antitoxin, 80
positioning, of patient, 71, 72, 73, 81
potato salad, 20–21
potato soup, cold, 11, 20
Pressure BioSciences, Inc., 47
pressure cycling technology (PCT), 47
prevention, 82–91
Project Bioshield, 113–114
prokaryotic cells, 30
proteins
  fingerprinting of, 107–109
  toxin action on, 38, 68
proteolytic toxins, 38, 68
Protista Kingdom, 28
Public Citizen, 102
public education, 82–83, 90, 119
Public Health Security and Bioterrorism
    Preparedness and Response Act (2002), 97
pupil measurement, 58

quorum sensing, 37

receptor-mediated endocytosis, 69
reemerging infections, 6
reference laboratories, 96, 101
refrigeration, 85, 86
Regal Swan project, 115–116
respiratory failure, 71–72, 81
retina measurement, 58
reverse Trendelenburg position, 72, 73, 81
ribonucleic acid (RNA), 112–113
ribosomes, 34, 112
riboswitches, 112–113

ribozymes, 112
RNA detection, 112–113

Salmonella, 46, 94
Sandia National Laboratories, 107
Sanger Institute, 95
Sarin, 38
sausage poisoning, 16–17
scratch test, 76–77
sensory neuron, 64
sentinel laboratories, 96, 98–100
serum
  horse, antitoxin development from, 74
  testing of, 51, 57
serum sickness, 76, 79
shellfish poisoning, 53, 70
shock, 74, 75, 76, 79, 119
skin testing, for antitoxin use, 76–77
smallpox, 94
Smith, Leonard A., 117
SNAP-25, 67–69
SNARE proteins, 67–69
somatic nervous system, 62, 63
Soviet Union, 93
spasticity, toxin for, 60–61, 115
spinal tap, 54, 55
spirilli, 32
spores. *See* endospores
Sporolactobacillus, 34
Sporosarcina, 34
sporulation, 34, 35, 36
Sprague, Lori, 103
stain, bacteria, 31, 32
Stanford University, 103–106
Stanker, Larry, 48
stomach, pumping of, 72
Stonewall Kitchen, 25–26
stool specimen, 51, 57
strabismus, 60
strains, 37
Strategic National Stockpile, 81, 118
stroke
  in differential diagnosis, 53, 70
  toxin in treatment of, 60–61, 115
stuttering, 60–61
sudden infant death, 12, 17
Sulston, John, 109
swallowing difficulties, 71
Swaminathan, Subramanyam, 39, 40
swans, 115–116
sympathetic nervous system, 62, 63, 64
symptoms, 69
synaptic transmission, 66–68
synaptic vesicle, 66–68
syntaxin, 67–69

Tan, Weihong, 111
temperature, 28, 83, 84, 86–88, 106

tests, diagnostic, 54–58, 96, 110–112
test strip, 111–112
tic disorders, 60–61
tick paralysis, 53, 70
Ting, Edmund, 47
Tourette syndrome, 60–61
toxicities, *vs.* botulism, 53
toxin(s), 9–10, 37–40
  absorption of, 69
  action in nervous system, 68–70
  antitoxin for neutralizing, 46, 74–81, 82–83, 96, 118
  causing animal and bird disease, 12, 37, 38, 39
  causing human disease, 37, 39
  detection of, 46–48, 96, 107–113
  diffusion of, 69
  elimination from body, 72–74
  geographic distribution of, 9–10
  inhibitor of, 39, 114
  lethal nature of, 59
  medical uses of, 59, 60–61, 102–103, 115
  nerves affected by, 54, 69–70
  NIAID research on, 96
  paradox of, 114–115
toxin A, 37–39
  action of, 38–39, 68
  geographic distribution of, 9–10
  inhibitor of, 39
  medical uses of, 60–61, 102–103
toxin B, 37, 38, 39
  action of, 68
  geographic distribution of, 9, 10
  medical uses of, 60–61, 102–103
toxin C, 12, 37, 38, 39, 68
toxin C_2, 37
toxin D, 37, 38, 39, 68
toxin E, 37, 38, 39–40
  action of, 68
  geographic distribution of, 9
  structure of, 39–40
toxin F, 37, 38, 39, 68
toxin G, 10, 37, 68
toxoid, 75–76
trachea, 71
transmission
  of botulism, 41–49
  synaptic, 66–68
treatment, 71–81
  antitoxin, 46, 74–81, 82–83, 96
  breathing interventions, 71–72, 81
  clinical trials, 78, 79–81
  Project Bioshield and, 113–114

Trendelenburg position, reverse, 72, 73, 81
tricorder, 107
tularemia, 94, 101

Uganda, 23–24
Unit 731 (Japan), 92
University of Florida, 111
University of Georgia, 109–110
University of Maryland, 118
University of Nebraska at Lincoln, 117–118
urticaria, 76
USAMRIID. *See* U.S. Army Medical Research Institute of Infectious Diseases
U.S. Army, 80, 117–118
U.S. Army Medical Research Institute of Infectious Diseases (USAMRIID), 39–40, 97, 117–118
USDA. *See* Agriculture Department, U.S.
U.S. Geological Survey, 103

vaccines, advances in, 6–7
vaccines, botulism
  animal, 115–116, 119
  development of, 80–81, 114, 116–119
  Project Bioshield and, 113–114
ventilation, mechanical, 71–72, 81
vichyssoise, 11, 20
viral hemorrhagic fevers, 94
vocal tremors, 60–61
VX, 38

warning label, for Botox, 102
WB. *See* wound botulism
weapon, biological, 8, 14–15, 40, 92–101. *See also* bioterrorism
weaponization, 114–115
weck jars (weckglas), 86
windpipe (trachea), 71
Wood, Marcia, 47
World Health Organization (WHO), 85–86
worms, for chemical testing, 109–110
wound botulism (WB), 12
  incidence of, 8–9
  increase in, 24
  prevention of, 89
  treatment of, 71–81
wound/tissue specimen, 51
wrinkles, 60–61

Yellowstone National Park, 30

ZVED. *See* National Center for Zoonotic, Vector-Borne, and Enteric Disease

About the Author

Dr. Donald Emmeluth spent most of his teaching career in upstate New York. In 1999, Dr. Emmeluth retired from the State University of New York system and became a member of the Biology Department of Armstrong Atlantic State University in Savannah. At AASU, Dr. Emmeluth teaches and coordinates the Principles of Biology course. He also teaches Microbiology, Microorganisms and Disease, Environmental Biology, and a special topics course in BioEthics. He developed and maintains the Biology Department Web site.

He has published several journal articles and is the co-author of a high school biology textbook. He has also authored three other books in this series: *Influenza*, *Typhoid Fever*, and *Plague*.

He has served as president of the National Association of Biology Teachers (NABT). During his career, Dr. Emmeluth has received a number of honors and awards, including the Chancellor's Award for Excellence in Teaching from the State University of New York system and the Two-Year College Biology Teaching Award from NABT. In 2003, Dr. Emmeluth was awarded NABT's Honorary Membership Award for outstanding contributions to Biology and Life Science Education. This award is the association's highest honor.

About the Consulting Editor

Hilary Babcock, M.D., M.P.H., is an assistant professor of medicine at Washington University School of Medicine and the medical director of occupational health for Barnes-Jewish Hospital and St. Louis Children's Hospital. She received her undergraduate degree from Brown University and her M.D. from the University of Texas Southwestern Medical Center at Dallas. After completing her residency, chief residency, and Infectious Disease fellowship at Barnes-Jewish Hospital, she joined the faculty of the Infectious Disease division. She completed an M.P.H. in Public Health from St. Louis University School of Public Health in 2006. She has lectured, taught, and written extensively about infectious diseases, their treatment, and their prevention. She is a member of numerous medical associations and is board certified in infectious disease. She lives in St. Louis, Missouri.

Grandpa Loved

BY JOSEPHINE NOBISSO · ILLUSTRATED BY MAUREEN HYDE

Gingerbread House
Westhampton Beach, New York

Gingerbread House
602 Montauk Highway
Westhampton Beach
New York 11978

1 (631) 288-5119
Fax 1 (631) 288-5179
e-mail: ghbooks@optonline.net
www.gingerbreadbooks.com

Original version published by The Green Tiger Press
Subsequently published by Simon & Schuster
Gingerbread House SAN: 217-0760

Printed in Hong Kong
Manufactured by Regent Publishing Services Ltd.

Revised 2000
10 9 8 7 6 5 4 3 2 1

Publisher's Cataloging-in-Publication *(Provided by Quality Books, Inc.)*
Nobisso, Josephine.
Grandpa loved / by Josephine Nobisso;
illustrated by Maureen Hyde. -- 2nd ed.
p. cm.
SUMMARY: Grandpa's love of life insures that he
is still present, after his death, in the lives of all who loved
him.
LCCN: 99-75393
ISBN: 0-940112-04-3
1. Grandfathers--Juvenile fiction.
2. Grandfathers--Death--Juvenile fiction. 3. Death--Juvenile
fiction.
4. Grief in children--Juvenile fiction. 5. Bereavement in children--
Juvenile fiction.
I. Hyde, Maureen, ill. II. Title.

545Gs 2000   [E]
                    QBI99-1372

That's what Grandpa loved most about the city—hearing all those lives.

We let any lost and lonely person tell us a life's story. Grandpa said that his being so old and my being so young made it easy for people to tell us so much.

We built a manger where deer and raccoons and birds came to eat our bread and corn and garden greens. Grandpa said that woodland creatures are so sensitive they can feel any nervousness around them.

That's what Grandpa loved most about the woods—being so calm and easy with all those animals.

We tumbled on soft moist moss, and tunneled into drifts of dry leaves.

Grandpa loved the city where we live. He taught me to love it, too. We let the dusty warm scent in museums carry us away, and the quiet buzz of the library lull us to doze.

To Grandpa Ralph and his four girls:
Nicolle, Gina, Bianca, and Kali Marie
—J.N.

For my father, with special thanks
to Russ, Jake and Sam.
—M.H.

Grandpa loved to stand on the beach.
He showed me how to love it, too.

We let the ocean foam creep up our legs, and the sun squint our eyes. We let the sea air breathe us–in and out, in and out–very deeply, very friendly.

Grandpa said that the earth was hurtling
through space so fast it sent winds
across the planet.

That's what Grandpa loved most about the beach—catching all that wind.

Grandpa loved the woods behind the summer house. He planted that love in me too.

Grandpa loved the people in our family.
He grew that love in me, too.

We danced at weddings, and sang at parties. We played with the new babies, and visited the sick.

Grandpa said that people who died could
go anywhere, at any time. That must be what
Grandpa loves most now–being with us
everywhere, all the time–on the beach, in the
country, and in the city–in the lives of all who
loved him.